FOURTH EDITION

WORLD LINK 1

DEVELOPING ENGLISH FLUENCY

JAMES R. MORGAN

NANCY DOUGLAS

NATIONAL GEOGRAPHIC
LEARNING

Australia · Brazil · Canada · Mexico · Singapore · United Kingdom · United States

National Geographic Learning,
a Cengage Company

World Link Level 1: Developing English Fluency, **Fourth Edition**

Publisher: Sherrise Roehr

Executive Editor: Sarah Kenney

Senior Development Editor: Lewis Thompson

Director of Global Marketing: Ian Martin

Heads of Regional Marketing:
  Charlotte Ellis (Europe, Middle East and Africa)
  Irina Pereyra (Latin America)

Senior Product Marketing Manager:
  Caitlin Thomas

Content Project Manager: Beth Houston

Media Researcher: Stephanie Eenigenburg

Cover/Text Design: Lisa Trager

Art Director: Brenda Carmichael

Operations Support: Hayley Chwazik-Gee,
  Avi Mednick, Katie Lee

Manufacturing Planner: Mary Beth Hennebury

Composition: MPS North America LLC

For permission to use material from this text or product, submit all requests online at **cengage.com/permissions**
Further permissions questions can be emailed to
permissionrequest@cengage.com

Student's Book
ISBN: 978-0-357-50213-6
Student's Book + My World Link Online:
ISBN: 978-0-357-50214-3

National Geographic Learning
200 Pier 4 Boulevard
Boston, MA 02210
USA

Locate your local office at **international.cengage.com/region**

Visit National Geographic Learning online at **ELTNGL.com**
Visit our corporate website at **www.cengage.com**

Printed in China
Print Number: 02 Print Year: 2021

Acknowledgments

Thank you to the educators who provided invaluable feedback throughout the development of the *World Link* series:

Asia

Michael Jake Arcilla, Aii Language Center, Phnom Penh; Fintan Brennan, Meisei University, Tokyo; Tyler Burden, Meisei University, Tokyo; Catherine Cheetham, Tokai University, Tokyo; Will Fan, Xiamen Wanda, Xiamen; Mark Firth, Oberlin University, Machida; Hiroshi Fukuda, Jumonji University, Niiza; Thomas Goetz, Hokusei Gakuen University, Sapporo; Helen Hanae, Reitaku University, Kashiwa; Louis Liu, Meten English, Shenzen; Shaun McLewin, Hanseo University, Seosan; Raymond Monk, Jr., Meten English, Dalian; Donald Patterson, Seirei Christopher University, Hamamatsu City; Mongkol Sodachan, Rangsit University, Pathum Thani; Robert Wright, Meten English, Chengdu; Elvira Wu, Meten English, Quanzhou; I-Cheng Wu, Southern Taiwan University of Science and Technology, Tainan City; Xie Yu, SFLEP, Shanghai; Vince Zhang, Thinktown, Hangzhou; Vivi Zhang, Xiamen Wanda, Xiamen

Latin America

Anthony Acevedo, ICPNA, Lima; Jorge Aguilar, Centro de Estudios de Idiomas UAS, Culiacan; Lidia Stella Aja, Centro Cultural Colombo Americano, Cali; Ana Laura Alferez, Instituto Domingo Savio, Mexico City; Lúcia Rodrigues Alves, Seven, Sao Paulo; Alessandra Atarcsay, WOWL Education, Rio de Janeiro; Isabella Campos Alvim, IBEU Copacabana, Rio de Janeiro; Ana Berg, Ana Berg EFL School, Rio de Janeiro; Raul Billini, Santo Domingo; Isabela Villas Boas, Casa Thomas Jefferson, Brasilia; Lourdes Camarillo, Escuela Bancaria Comercial, Mexico City; Cinthia Castañeda, Centro de Idiomas, Coatzacoalcos; Enrique Chapuz, Universidad Veracruzana, Coatzacoalcos; Giseh Cuesta, MESCyT, Mexico City; Carlos Fernández, ICPNA, Lima; Vania Furtado, IBEU Copacabana, Rio de Janeiro; Mariana Garcia, BUAP, Puebla; Jeanette Bravo Garonce, IPA Idiomas, Brasilia; Luiz Henrique Bravo Garonce, IPA Idiomas, Brasilia; Fily Hernandez, Universidad Veracruzana, Coatzacoalcos; Manuel Hidalgo Iglesias, Escuela Bancaria Comercial, Mexico City; Dafna Ilian, ESIME, Azcapotzalco; Rubén Jacome, Universidad Veracruzana, Coatzacoalcos; Beatriz Jorge, Alumni, Sao Paulo; Gledis Libert, ICDA, Santo Domingo; Rocio Liceaga, International House, Mexico City; Elizabeth Palacios, ICPNA, Lima; Emeli Borges Pereira Luz, UNICAMPI, Sao Paulo; Patricia McKay, CELLEP, Sao Paulo; Victor Hugo Medina, Cultura Inglesa Minas Gerais, Belo Horizonte; Maria Helena Meyes, ACBEU, Salvador; Isaias Pacheco, Universidad Veracruzana, Coatzacoalcos; Miguel Rodriguez, BUAP, Puebla; Nelly Romero, ICPNA, Lima; Yesenia Ruvalcaba, Universidad de Guadalajara, Guadalajara; Eva Sanchez, BUAP, Puebla; Marina Sánchez, Instituto Domingo Savio, Mexico City; Thais Scharfenberg, Centro Europeu, Curitiba; Pilar Sotelo, ICPNA, Lima; Rubén Uceta, Centro Cultural Domínico Americano, Santiago De Los Caballeros; Italia Vergara, American English Overseas Center, Panama City; Maria Victoria Guinle Vivacqua, UNICAMP, Sao Paulo

United States and Canada

Bobbi Plante, Manitoba Institute of Trades and Technology, Winnipeg; Richard McDorman, Language On Schools, Miami, FL; Luba Nesteroba, Bilingual Education Institute, Houston, TX; Tracey Partin, Valencia College, Orlando, FL

SCOPE AND SEQUENCE

PRONUNCIATION	SPEAKING	READING	WRITING	ACTIVE ENGLISH	LISTENING AND READING SKILLS	GLOBAL VOICES
Question intonation p. 4	Introducing yourself and asking questions p. 6	How to Spot a Fake Photo p. 10	Write a description of a photo p. 14	Ask questions to gather personal information p. 8 Talk about and describe people p. 14	Listen for details p. 5 Check understanding p. 10	Nice to Meet You p. 15
Contractions p. 20	Greeting people and asking how they are p. 20	What Are You Afraid Of? p. 24	Write about feelings p. 28	Create conversations based on an image p. 22 Game to explore classmates' feelings p. 28	Make predictions p. 25 Understand meaning p. 26	How Do You Feel? p. 29
Syllables p. 33	Talking about things you need p. 34	A Magical Market p. 38	Write about a favorite store p. 42	Find ingredients for a dish p. 36 Talk about what someone has and needs p. 42	Check comprehension p. 38 Understand context p. 40	At the Market p. 43
Sentence stress p. 53	Giving and responding to advice p. 50	Getting Ready! Packing tips for your next trip p. 54	Write an email p. 58	Create a visitor's guide p. 52 Plan a trip p. 58	Make predictions p. 49 Identify topic sentences p. 55	National Geographic Explorers: What Item Would You Not Leave Home Without? p. 59
Simple past -ed endings p. 71	Agreeing and disagreeing with an opinion p. 64	Pay it Forward p. 68	Write a letter to nominate someone for an award p. 72	Talk about interesting people from the past p. 66 Talk about helpful people p. 72	Identify sequences p. 63 Use existing knowledge p. 69	Our Hero: Jane Goodall p. 73
Irregular simple past p. 79	Expressing degrees of certainty p. 78	A Study of Sleep p. 82	Write about a past experience p. 86	Talk about an important event from the past p. 80 Talk about sleep habits and give advice p. 86	Listen for details p. 77 Identify the main idea p. 83	Neil deGrasse Tyson: How Many Hours Do You Sleep? p. 87

SCOPE AND SEQUENCE

PRONUNCIATION	SPEAKING	READING	WRITING	ACTIVE ENGLISH	LISTENING AND READING SKILLS	GLOBAL VOICES
Stress in compound nouns p. 93	Asking for and giving directions p. 94	Let's Go on the Metro! p. 98	Write about things to do and see in a city p. 102	Use logic to solve a crime p. 96 Make a plan for someone with 24 hours in a city p. 102	Summarize p. 99 Listen for context p. 100	Getting around Seoul p. 103
Reduced *to* and *want to* p. 109	Inviting others to do something p. 108	Life Style p. 112	Write a personal profile p. 116	Conduct a survey of classmates' interests p. 110 Share an interesting fact about yourself p. 116	Listen for details p. 107 Personalize p. 112	Malaika Vaz: All about Me p. 117
Contracted *would* p. 123	Making and responding to requests p. 122	From Hero to Zero p. 126	Write a plan for the future p. 130	Talk about a personal habit to break p. 124 Discuss plastic in a morning routine p. 130	Understand context p. 121 Make predictions p. 126	Melati Wijsen: Changemaker p. 131
Vowel length p. 138	Talking about health problems p. 138	Less Stress Before Your Next Big Test p. 142	Write about a past experience with stress p. 146	Create a poster to give health advice p. 140 Make a plan to have less stress p. 146	Listen for signposts p. 137 Apply understanding p. 143	Let's Talk about Stress p. 147
Can / can't, could / couldn't p. 153	Complimenting someone on ability p. 152	A Brave Pilot p. 156	Write about a hope for the future p. 160	Interview a classmate about their talents p. 154 Talk about things on a bucket list p. 160	Test comprehension p. 151 Apply ideas p. 157	National Geographic Explorers: My Proudest Accomplishment p. 161
Sentence stress p. 167	Talking on the phone p. 166	A Movie Remake p. 170	Write a movie review p. 174	Create a movie poster p. 168 Discuss favorite movies p. 174	Listen for signposts p. 165 Discuss findings p. 171	My Favorite Movie p. 175

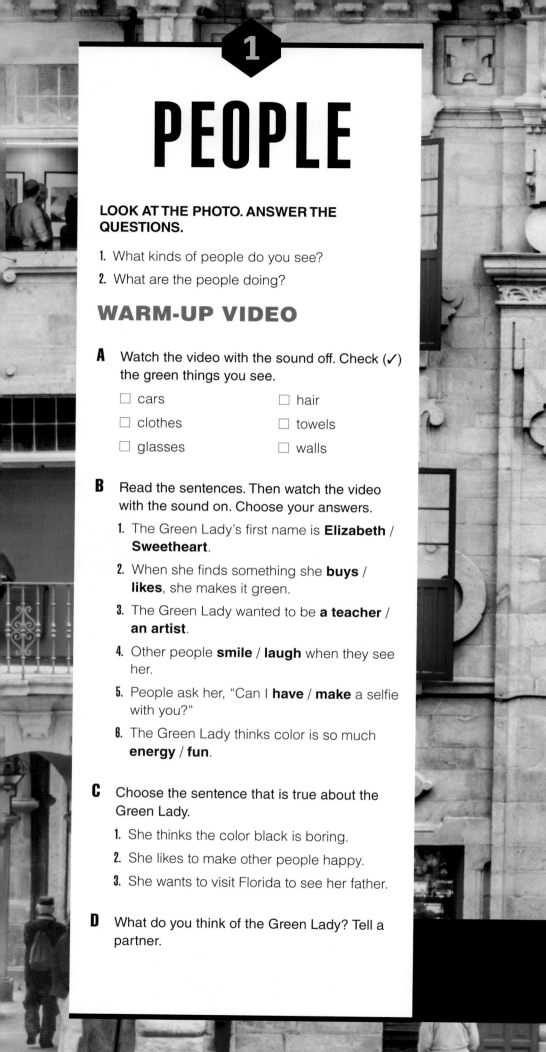

1

PEOPLE

LOOK AT THE PHOTO. ANSWER THE QUESTIONS.

1. What kinds of people do you see?
2. What are the people doing?

WARM-UP VIDEO

A Watch the video with the sound off. Check (✓) the green things you see.

☐ cars   ☐ hair

☐ clothes   ☐ towels

☐ glasses   ☐ walls

B Read the sentences. Then watch the video with the sound on. Choose your answers.

1. The Green Lady's first name is **Elizabeth** / **Sweetheart**.

2. When she finds something she **buys** / **likes**, she makes it green.

3. The Green Lady wanted to be **a teacher** / **an artist**.

4. Other people **smile** / **laugh** when they see her.

5. People ask her, "Can I **have** / **make** a selfie with you?"

6. The Green Lady thinks color is so much **energy** / **fun**.

C Choose the sentence that is true about the Green Lady.

1. She thinks the color black is boring.

2. She likes to make other people happy.

3. She wants to visit Florida to see her father.

D What do you think of the Green Lady? Tell a partner.

People visit an art exhibition in Spain.

5

GOALS

VOCABULARY

A Look at Silvia's profile. Practice saying the words in **blue**.

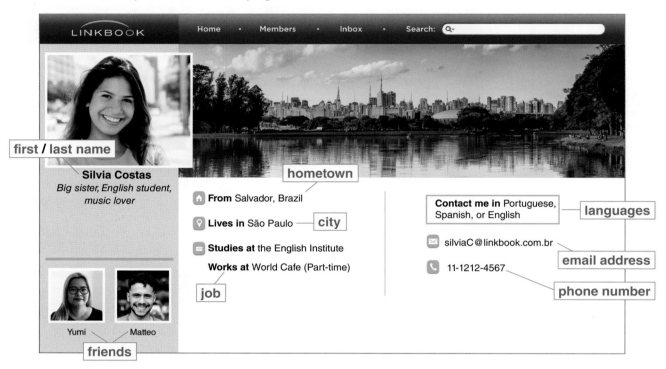

B Work with a partner. Complete the questions and answers about Silvia with the words in **blue** from **A**.

1. What's her _____? (It's) Silvia.
2. What's her _____? (It's) Costas.
3. What's her _____ number? (It's) 11-1212-4567.
4. What's her _____ address? (It's) silviaC@linkbook.com.br.
5. Where is she from? She's from Salvador. It's her _____.
6. Where does she live now? She lives in São Paulo. It's a big _____!
7. What does she do? She's a student, and she has a part-time _____.
8. How many _____ does she speak? She speaks three languages: Portuguese, Spanish, and English.
9. What does she do for fun? She's in a band with her _____, Yumi and Matteo.

ℹ Saying Email Addresses

silviaC@linkbook.com.br = silvia C (at) linkbook (dot) com (dot) b-r

C PRONUNCIATION: Question Intonation Read the questions. Then listen and repeat. Notice the intonation. 🎧 2

What's your name? What do you do? Where do you live now?

D Interview a partner. Use the questions in **B** as a model.

LISTENING

A An interviewer is asking people questions at a festival in South Korea. Listen.
Then write the missing words. 🎧3

Conversation 1 What's _____?

Where are _____?

Conversation 2 _____ speaking German?

What do _____?

_____ languages do you speak?

_____ are you interested in?

Conversation 3 _____ are you from?

_____ your plan for today?

B **Listen for details.** Listen again. Complete the chart with each person's
job and city only. Write *NM* for information that is not mentioned. 🎧3

WORD BANK
I'm **interested in** Korean
music and culture.

	Job	City	Interest
Person 1			
Person 2			
Person 3			

C What is each person interested in at the festival? Write your answers in **B**.
Then listen one more time and check your answers 🎧3

66 I'm interested in
the food. What
about you?

D Imagine you can go to the festival. What are you interested in? Tell a partner.

**People can try food from all over the world at the Global Village
Festival in Seoul, South Korea.**

A student plays a guitar in Washington Square Park in New York City, US—the location of Hunter College and New York University (NYU).

SPEAKING

A Read the conversation and listen. Are Danny and Mariana meeting for the first time? How do you know? 🎧4

Mariana: Hi. My name is Mariana. I'm in apartment 201.

Danny: Hi, Mariana. I'm Danny. I'm in 302. It's nice to meet you.

Mariana: Nice to meet you, too.

Danny: So, are you a student, Mariana?

Mariana: Yeah, I study music at NYU.

Danny: That's interesting.

Mariana: What do you do, Danny?

Danny: I'm a student at Hunter College. I also work in an art gallery.

B Practice the conversation in **A** with a partner. Then practice with your own information.

C Introduce yourself to four classmates. Ask them about their jobs and complete the chart. Use the Speaking Strategy to help you.

Name	Job
Mariana	music student

D Tell a partner about the classmates you talked to in **C**.

SPEAKING STRATEGY 🎧5
Introducing Yourself and Asking Questions

Introducing Yourself	Asking Questions
A: My name is Mariana. **B:** Hi, I'm Danny. (It's) Nice to meet you. **A:** (It's) Nice to meet you, too.	**A:** What do you do? **B:** I'm a music student.
When you are introducing yourself, *My name is . . .* and *I'm . . .* can both be used.	

❝ Mariana is a student.
She studies music.

GRAMMAR

A Read the Unit 1, Lesson A Grammar Reference in the appendix. Complete the exercises. Then do the exercises below.

REVIEW OF THE SIMPLE PRESENT		
	Questions	**Answers**
Yes / No Questions with *Be*	**Are** you a student? **Is** he a student?	Yes, I **am**. / No, I'm not. Yes, he **is**. / No, he's not.
Yes / No Questions with Other Verbs	**Do** you **speak** English? **Does** she **speak** English?	Yes, I **do**. / No, I **don't**. Yes, she **does**. / No, she **doesn't**.
Wh- Questions	What do you do? What does she do?	I'm a student. She's a doctor.

B Read Steffi's paragraph. Write the correct form of each verb.

Monika (1.) _____is_____ (be) my classmate. We (2.) _____ (be) different in many ways. I (3.) _____ (be) an only child. Monika (4.) _____ (have) two brothers and a sister. I (5.) _____ (live) with my family. Monika (6.) _____ (live) in her own apartment. We both go to Western University. I (7.) _____ (study) English literature. Monika (8.) _____ (study) business. I (9.) _____ (not have) a job, but Monika (10.) _____ (work) part-time in a cafe. I (11.) _____ (love) dance music, but Monika (12.) _____ (not like) it. She (13.) _____ (listen) to rap. Monika and I (14.) _____ (watch) TV together on the weekends.

C Complete questions 1–4 with the correct form of *be* or *do*. Complete questions 5–8 with a *Wh-* question word. Then take turns asking and answering the questions with a partner.

1. _____ Steffi and Monika different?
2. _____ Steffi an only child?
3. _____ Steffi study business?
4. _____ Monika and Steffi go to the same university?

5. _____ subject does Steffi study?
6. _____ does Monika work?
7. _____ does Steffi live with?
8. _____ does Monika live?

D Complete each sentence with the affirmative or negative form of a verb from the box to make it true for you.

> **WORD BANK**
> My favorite **subject** is math.

have	like	speak	study

1. I _____ a middle name.
2. I _____ my first name.
3. I _____ more than one language well.

4. I _____ on the weekend.
5. I _____ my hometown.
6. I _____ a favorite subject at school.

E How are you and your partner similar and different? Use your sentences in **D** to form questions. Ask follow-up questions.

"" Do you have a middle name?

Yes, I do. ""

"" What is it?

It's Victor. ""

Lesson A | **7**

The *Inside Out* project by French Artist JR allows people to share their own photo in a large artwork. Here, people share their photos in Shanghai, China.

ACTIVE ENGLISH Try it out!

A Ask each question in the chart until you find a person who answers *Yes*. Write their name. Then ask one follow-up question and write the extra information.

i Follow-up Questions

Follow-up questions are an important part of conversation. *Wh-* questions allow you to get more information than *Yes / No* questions.

Find someone who . . .	Name	Extra Information
1. has a part-time job.		
2. speaks three languages.		
3. says their favorite subject is math.		
4. is interested in English.		
5. likes their hometown.		
6. knows a friend's email address.		
7. doesn't like big cities.		
8. eats breakfast every day.		

B Tell a classmate about the people in your chart.

❝ Nicholas doesn't like big cities. He doesn't like the noise.

1A **GOALS**	Now I can . . .

Introduce myself and share personal information _____

Ask about a person's job _____

1. Yes, I can.
2. Mostly, yes.
3. Not yet.

VOCABULARY

A Complete the sentences about the people in the photo. Use the words in the Word Bank. Then tell a partner about each person.

1. Albert Lin is a scientist. He is _____ weight. He has _____, _____ hair.

2. Ami Vitale is a photographer. She has _____, _____ hair.

3. Ronan Donovan is a photographer. He's not short. He's _____. He's not heavy. He's _____.

4. Kimberly Jeffries is a diver. Her hair isn't curly. It's _____. She has _____ eyes.

5. Renan Ozturk is a rock climber. He was born in 1980. I think that's _____.

B Choose four or five words from the Word Bank. Tell a partner about yourself.

❝ I have brown hair and green eyes.

I'm average height. **❞**

C Who do you look like? Tell a partner.

❝ I look like my cousin. We have the same color eyes and the same hairstyle.

ℹ Word Order

Notice the word order to describe appearance: *long* (size), *blond* (color) *hair*

WORD BANK

Be + . . .	Have + . . .	
young / old in your teens in your twenties	brown / blue / green	eyes
thin average weight heavy	long ↔ short straight ↔ curly	hair
short average height tall	black / brown blond / red	hair
look like to be similar in appearance to		

Albert Lin

Ronan Donovan

Ami Vitale

Kimberly Jeffries

Renan Ozturk

HOW TO SPOT A **FAKE PHOTO**

Look at the three photos. The woman at the top has long, black hair. She is wearing glasses. She is also wearing earrings. The woman in the middle has curly, black hair. She has brown eyes. She is in her thirties. The woman at the bottom has blond hair. She's young. She is in her twenties. She has green eyes.

One of the photos shows a real person. Two of the photos do not show real people. The photos are from a computer, and they are fake.

Some people use computers to make fake photos of other people. They scan millions of photos of real faces and then make new ones.

It can be difficult to tell the difference[1] between a real photo and a fake photo. Here are some things to look for:

Look closely at the left and right sides of a person's glasses. In some fake photos, they don't match. They're different.

Also, a person's two earrings and eyes can be different in a fake photo.

Finally, in a fake photo, the background[2] can be strange. It doesn't look right.

Look at the three photos again. Which two are fake? How do you know?

[1] If you can **tell the difference**, you can see that two things are not the same.
[2] The **background** is the area behind the person or thing in a photo.

A Describe the people in the photos in your own words.

B Read the first paragraph of the article. Are your descriptions in **A** the same?

C **Check understanding.** Find the words in the article. Choose the correct answers.

1. *They are fake* means . . .
   a. they aren't real.
   b. they are from a computer.

2. *Look closely* means . . .
   a. look for a short time.
   b. look for a long time.

3. *They don't match* means . . .
   a. they are the same.
   b. they aren't the same.

D Read the rest of the article. Choose **T** for *true* or **F** for *false*.

1. One of the photos is real.　　　　**T**　　**F**

2. You can use computers to make fake photos. T F

3. It is easy to tell the difference between real and fake photos. T F

4. A person's glasses or earrings may not match in a fake photo. T F

5. The background looks the same in real and fake photos. T F

E Work with a partner. Which photos are fake? Take turns. Give your reasons. Check your answer at the bottom of the page.

Answer E: The top photo is fake. The two sides of the glasses and the ears are different. The bottom photo is also fake. The background looks strange.

LISTENING

A The words in the box describe a person's appearance. Do you know what they mean? Listen. Then practice saying them with your teacher. 🎧7

> good-looking   handsome   petite   pretty

B Listen to the first part of a podcast. Complete the sentences. 🎧8

My name is Emi, and this is English Express: a short, daily podcast about (1.) _____. Today, we're talking about describing people's appearance—how they (2.) _____. Is a person tall or (3.) _____? Do they have brown hair or (4.) _____ hair? Are they wearing (5.) _____? There are many ways to describe a person's appearance.

WORD BANK
A: Can you **describe** her?
B: Sure. She's tall and wears glasses.
Some men grow a **beard** or **mustache**.

C Listen to the complete podcast. Who do the words describe? Write **M** for *men*, **W** for *women*, or **B** for *both*. 🎧9

1. _____ good-looking
2. _____ handsome
3. _____ pretty
4. _____ petite

D Complete the sentences. Give reasons for your choices.

I think _____ is handsome / pretty.

My reason: _____

I think _____ is handsome / pretty.

My reason: _____

E Interview five classmates. Find out who they think is handsome and pretty. Take notes on their answers.

❝ In your opinion, who is handsome?

I think . . . is handsome. ❞

❝ Really? Why?

He's tall and has a beard. ❞

F Work with a partner. Look at your notes from **E**. Complete 1 and 2. Then discuss 3.

1. In your notebook, make a list of men your class thinks are handsome.

2. In your notebook, make a list of women your class thinks are pretty.

3. Why are these people popular?

You don't have to be perfect to be pretty. Princess Eugenie of the British Royal Family wears a wedding dress that reveals a scar on her back.

GRAMMAR

A Read the Unit 1, Lesson B Grammar Reference in the appendix. Complete the exercises. Then do the exercises below.

DESCRIBING APPEARANCE			
Subject	*Be / Have*	Adjective	Noun
He	is	tall.	
		average	height / weight.
		young / in his teens.	
	has	blue	eyes.
		long / straight / black	hair.

B Work with a partner. Practice the conversation. Can you guess the person? Check your answer at the bottom of the page.

A: I'm thinking of a famous person.

B: Is it a woman?

A: No, it's a man.

B: Is he British?

A: No, he's not. He's from Argentina.

B: Is he tall?

A: No, he's not. He's a little short.

B: Is he in his twenties?

A: No, I think he's in his thirties.

B: Does he have long hair?

A: No, he doesn't.

B: Is he a soccer player?

A: Yes, he is.

B: I know! It's . . .

C Think of a famous person. Complete the notes. Do not show them to anyone.

Name:	Eyes:
Job:	Age:
Nationality:	Height:
Hair:	Weight:

D Work with a partner. Ask seven *Yes / No* questions about their famous person. Write down the information you learn.

1. _____
2. _____
3. _____
4. _____
5. _____
6. _____
7. _____

E Guess your partner's famous person.

Answer B: Lionel Messi!

ACTIVE ENGLISH Try it out!

A Look at the photo. Choose two of the people. Write key words about their appearance.

	Person 1	Person 2
Body		
Hair		
Height		

WORD BANK
have +
~ a nice smile
~ a friendly face
be +
~ in great shape

B Work with a partner. Complete the task. Then change roles.

Student A: Tell your partner about one of the people. Start each sentence with *This person* . . . Use your notes from **A**.

Student B: Which person is it? Guess.

C Work on your own. Find a personal photo with people in it. Make notes about the questions.

1. Who is in the photo?

2. Where are the people in the photo?

3. What does each person look like? Describe them.

D Work with a new partner. Take turns asking and answering questions about your photos.

66 | This is a photo of me and my father in 2013. We're in the mountains. My father is tall and has . . .

How old are you there? 99

E Look again at your partner's photo. Answer the three questions in **C**. Can you remember the answers?

66 | About ten years old.

F **WRITING** Write a description of your photo. Turn to the Writing appendix to see an example. Then use your notes from **C** to write your description.

| 1B | GOALS | Now I can . . . |

Describe a person's appearance _____
Describe myself _____

1. Yes, I can.
2. Mostly, yes.
3. Not yet.

Lucy (far left) and Maria (far right) Alymer with their family. Lucy and Maria look different, but they are twins!

GLOBAL VOICES

A Watch the speakers in Lima, Peru. Which country is each person from? Complete the sentences.

> Brazil   Colombia   Peru

1. Laura *is from Colombia* _____.
2. Abel _____.
3. Yasbeth _____.
4. Igor _____.

B Choose the correct answer(s).

1. Abel likes **salsa music** / **soccer** / **to run**.
2. Yasbeth likes **salsa music** / **soccer** / **to run**.

C Watch the speakers in Lisbon, Portugal. Match them with the languages they speak.

Usani

Adrià

Catalan
English
French
Portuguese
Russian
Spanish

D Choose the question that best matches what the speakers in China say.

1. What do you do for fun?

2. How many languages do you speak?

E Think about your own answer to the question you chose in **D**. Then tell a partner.

People from lots of different countries live in Lisbon, Portugal.

BEHAVIOR

LOOK AT THE PHOTO. ANSWER THE QUESTIONS.

1. What are the people doing?
2. Why are they doing this?

WARM-UP VIDEO

A Look up the words *smile* and *happy* in a dictionary. Then smile for a partner.

B Read the sentences and choose your own answers. Choose **T** for *true* and **F** for *false*.

1. When people are happy, they smile.   **T   F**
2. When you smile, you start to feel   **T   F**
   happy.

C Watch the video. Check your answers in **B**.

D Watch the video again. Complete each sentence with one word.

1. The same is true of how you _____ and . . . walk.
2. If you put energy into your voice and a spring in your step, you'll . . . _____ much better.

E Try the smile test for 30 seconds. Then complete the task.

1. Read the second sentence in **B**. Was this true for you?
2. Read the sentences in **D**. Do you agree?

Fans watch a game during the Rugby World Cup in Cape Town, South Africa.

GOALS

Lesson A

/ Greet people and ask how they are

/ Talk about actions happening now and these days

Lesson B

/ Explain how you feel

/ Talk about things you are afraid of

A group of students at the Color Run in Shenzhen, China

VOCABULARY

A Say the verbs in the Word Bank with your teacher. Which ones do you know? Watch your teacher perform each action.

WORD BANK

laugh	start
look	stop
run	watch
shout	wave
smile	wear

B Work with a partner. Look at the photo. Where are the people?

C Read the sentences. Choose the ones that are true.

1. a. They're **looking** at the camera.   b. They're **watching** the race.
2. a. They're **running** in the race.   b. They're **stopping** for a photo.
3. a. They're **wearing** the same glasses.   b. They're **wearing** the same shirts.

D Match each sentence (1–4) to a person in the photo. Write the number.

1. She's **laughing**.   2. He's **smiling**.   3. She's **waving**.   4. He's **shouting**.

E Work with a partner. Cover the sentences in **C** and **D**. What's happening in the photo? Take turns explaining.

" Some students are at the Color Run. They are standing together.

LISTENING

A Look at the photos. Why do the people have colored powder on their clothes? Guess.

B Read the sentences. Then listen and choose **T** for *true* or **F** for *false*. 🎧10

1. The man is running with his family.   **T**   **F**
2. At the starting line, the man sees many people.   **T**   **F**
3. All of the people the man can see are running in the race.   **T**   **F**
4. In the park, people are throwing water.   **T**   **F**
5. At the finish line, people are shouting and waving.   **T**   **F**

> **WORD BANK**
> You can **throw** something in your hands at another person or thing.

C Listen again. Correct the false sentences in **B** in your notebook. 🎧10

D Listen. Write a number or word to complete the information. 🎧11

The Color Run happens in over (1.) _____ countries. It's
(2.) _____ kilometers. There is (3.) _____ rule:
everyone has to wear a (4.) _____ T-shirt. There are
(5.) _____ winners or losers in the race. People do it for
(6.) _____.

E Answer the questions with a partner.

1. What happens at the Color Run?
2. Do you think the Color Run is a fun activity? Why or why not?

The Color Run happens in lots of different countries, like here, in England.

Taking a break is important when you're busy and don't feel great.

SPEAKING

A Read the conversation and listen. How is Tomás? How is Carla? Why does she feel that way? 🎧12

Tomás: Hey, Carla.

Carla: Hi, Tomás. How's it going?

Tomás: OK. How are you doing?

Carla: So-so.

Tomás: Yeah? What's up?

Carla: Oh, I'm studying for a big test.

Tomás: Another test? You're working really hard these days.

Carla: I know!

Tomás: Do you want to stop and get some coffee?

Carla: That sounds good. Let's do it!

B **PRONUNCIATION: Contractions** Use contractions in spoken English. Notice that some expressions always use a contraction. Listen and say the sentences. 🎧13

1. How is it going? / **How's** it going?
2. I am studying. / **I'm** studying.
3. You are working hard. / **You're** working hard.
4. **What's** up?
5. **Let's** get (coffee).

C Practice the conversation in **A** with a partner. Then make a new conversation. Use the situations and the Speaking Strategy.

Situation 1
Student A: You feel ☺.
Student B: You feel ☹. You're doing homework. You have a lot.

Situation 2
Student A: You feel ☹. You're working extra hours at your part-time job.
Student B: You feel ☺.

D Greet four classmates and ask how they are. How are people in your class doing today?

SPEAKING STRATEGY 🎧14
Greeting People and Asking How They Are

☺	**A:** Hi, . . . How's it going? **B:** Fine. / OK. / All right. / Pretty good. How are you (doing)? **A:** I'm fine.
☹	**A:** Hi, . . . How are you doing? **B:** So-so. **A:** Yeah? What's up? **B:** I have a lot of homework.

GRAMMAR

A Read part of a conversation. Answer the questions.

A: I'm studying for a big test.

B: Another test? You're working really hard these days.

1. Which sentence is about something happening right now?

2. Which sentence is about something happening for a longer period of time in the present?

B Read the Unit 2, Lesson A Grammar Reference in the appendix. Complete the exercises. Then do the exercises below.

THE PRESENT CONTINUOUS: AFFIRMATIVE AND NEGATIVE STATEMENTS			
I'm / You're / She's / They're	(not)	**studying**	for a big test.
		working	hard these days.

YES / NO AND WH- QUESTIONS				
Question Word	*Be*		Verb + *-ing*	Answers
	Are	you		Yes, I am. / No, I'm not.
	Is	she	**studying?**	Yes, she is. / No, she's not.
	Are	they		Yes, they are. / No, they're not.
What	**are**	you		(I'm studying) English.
Where	**is**	she	**studying?**	(She's studying) at school.
Why	**are**	they		(They're studying) Because they have a test.

C Work with a partner. Use the words to complete the *Yes / No* questions with the present continuous.

1. _____Are you studying_____ (you / study) English for your job?

2. _____ (our classmate / wear) a sweater?

3. _____ (you / exercise) more these days?

4. _____ (your English / improve)?

5. _____ (people / travel) more nowadays?

6. _____ (our teacher / smile)?

D Work with your partner. Complete the task.

Student A: Ask your partner questions 1–3 from **C**. For each question, ask a follow-up *Wh-* question with the present continuous.

Student B: Answer with your opinion. Then change roles and ask questions 4–6 in **C**.

66 Are you studying English for your job?

No, I'm not. 99

66 Why are you studying English?

I'm preparing for an exam. 99

ACTIVE ENGLISH Try it out!

A Look at the picture. Where are the people? What are they doing?

B Work with a partner. Complete the conversation. Then practice it.

Mei: Felipe?

Felipe: Hi, Mei. (1.) _____ going?

Mei: Pretty (2.) _____. (3.) _____ doing?

Felipe: I'm fine. (4.) _____ (you, enjoy) the party?

Mei: Yes, (5.) _____. Thanks!

Felipe: So, (6.) _____ (you, live) in the school dorm this year, Mei?

Mei: No, (7.) _____.

Felipe: Really? (8.) _____ (you, live, where)?

Mei: (9.) _____ (a friend and I, rent) an apartment off campus.
Oh, and this is my roommate, Naoko. Naoko, this is Felipe.

C With your partner, choose two people from the picture. Make a conversation (8–10 sentences).
• Greet each other and ask how the other person is.
• Use three examples of the present continuous.

D Perform your conversation for another pair of students. Answer the questions when you listen.
1. Who is talking in the picture?
2. What are they talking about?

2A GOALS Now I can . . .

Greet people and ask how they are _____

Talk about actions happening now and these days _____

1. Yes, I can.
2. Mostly, yes.
3. Not yet.

VOCABULARY

A Say the words in blue. Watch your teacher perform each feeling.

afraid	nervous
angry	relaxed
bored	sad
excited	tired
happy	worried

B Look at the photos. How does each person feel? Guess. Then check your answers in the Information Gap Activities appendix.

1. a. happy   b. nervous

4. a. angry   b. relaxed

2. a. happy   b. tired

5. a. sad   b. afraid

3. a. excited   b. worried

6. a. excited   b. bored

C Work with a partner. Complete the task. Then change roles and repeat.

Student A: Choose six words in blue from **A**. Perform each feeling.

Student B: Close your book. Guess your partner's feelings.

D Answer the questions using the words in blue from **A**. Explain your answers.

How do you feel ...

- when you're waiting for the bus?
- when a friend is always late?
- before a big exam?
- when you speak English?
- about summer vacation?
- right now?

WHAT ARE YOU *AFRAID OF?*

Everyone is afraid of something. But what is *fear*,[1] and what can we do about it?

Fear can help *and* hurt us

We need fear to live. We see a big dog running at us, for example, and we feel afraid. This animal can hurt us, so we move away quickly. Other things can be dangerous:[2] swimming in deep water or driving a car fast. When we do these things, we feel afraid, so we are very careful doing them, or we stop doing them.

Some things aren't dangerous, but sometimes, we are afraid of them: talking in class, meeting other people, or taking an exam. We think something bad can happen, and then we feel worried. When we feel this way for a long time, it can hurt us.

Most fears are learned

Some things naturally scare[3] all people: loud sounds, falling, and some animals, like snakes and spiders. We learn to be afraid of everything else.

You can control your fear

To feel less afraid of something, ask these questions: *Why am I afraid of this thing?* and *What can I do about it?*

Don't run from your fear. Do something about it. Are you afraid to talk in class? Learn to do it. The more you do something, the more relaxed—and less afraid—you will feel.

[1] **Fear** is a strong nervous feeling. We feel it when something bad happens, or when we think it can happen.
[2] If something is **dangerous**, it can hurt you.
[3] When something **scares** you, it makes you feel afraid.

A trained bear roars at a group of boys in California, US.

A Complete the sentence so that it is true for you. Look up new words in a dictionary. Tell a partner your answer.

I'm afraid of _____.

- spiders
- swimming in deep water
- speaking English
- meeting new people
- other: _____

B **Make predictions.** Read the title, the subtitle, and the sentences in **bold**. Guess **T** for *true* and **F** for *false*.

1. Some people aren't afraid of anything.   T   F
2. Fear is always bad.   T   F
3. You can learn to be afraid of things.   T   F
4. You can change how you feel about a fear.   T   F

C Read the article. Then check your ideas in **B**.

D Work with a partner. Ask and answer the questions.

1. How does fear help us?
2. How does fear hurt us?
3. What things are all people afraid of?
4. To feel less afraid of something, what can you do?

E Look at your answer in **A**. Answer the three questions. Then tell your partner.

1. What are you afraid of?
2. Why are you afraid of it?
3. What can you do about it?

> **What are you afraid of?**   I'm afraid of swimming in deep water.

> **Why are you afraid of it?**   I can't swim well.

LISTENING

A Read sentences 1a–4a. Then listen. Choose the correct answers. 🎧16🎧

1. a. The woman feels **nervous** / **relaxed**.
   b. She ___know___ the information for her exams.

2. a. The man is very **angry** / **happy**.
   b. He's going to the ___world___ Cup.

3. a. The woman is **afraid** / **angry**.
   b. There's a ___spider___ in the kitchen.

4. a. The man is a little **bored** / **sad**.
   b. He misses the ___goodie___ back home.

B Listen again. Complete sentences 1b–4b. 🎧16🎧

C Listen one more time. Complete each expression with one word. 🎧16🎧

1. The man tells Ana, "Good _____!"

2. The man tells the woman, "I'm so _____!"

3. The man tells the woman, "Calm _____, please!"

4. The woman tells Chen, "Hang in _____."

> **WORD BANK**
> If you **miss** something, you are unhappy because it is not near you.

D **Understand meaning.** Match each expression in **C** (1–4) with its meaning (a–e). One answer is extra.

_____ a. Relax!

_____ b. I'm really happy!

_____ c. I don't know.

_____ d. Be strong. Things will be better soon.

_____ e. I hope you do well.

E Work with a partner. Complete the task.

1. Look again at the expressions in **C**. Are there similar expressions in your language?

2. Choose an expression from **C** and use it in a short conversation with your partner.

People on a roller coaster at an amusement park in Shanghai, China. How do they feel?

GRAMMAR

A Look at the pronouns in the chart. Read the sentences and choose the correct answers.

SUBJECT PRONOUNS		
Subject	Verb	Object
I	don't like	spiders.
You	don't like	spiders.
He / She	doesn't like	spiders.
We	don't like	spiders.
They	don't like	spiders.
It	is	a big dog.

OBJECT PRONOUNS		
Subject	Verb	Object
Spiders	scare	me.
Spiders	scare	you.
Spiders	scare	him / her.
Spiders	scare	us.
Spiders	scare	them.
I'm afraid of		it.

1. Object pronouns come **after** / **before** a verb.

2. **No** / **Two** object pronouns are the same as the subject pronouns.

B Read the Unit 2, Lesson B Grammar Reference in the appendix. Complete the exercises. Then do the exercises below.

C With a partner, complete the sentences with object pronouns. Notice the underlined words.

1. I speak <u>English</u> at school. I speak _____it_____ outside class, too.

2. When I speak English, <u>I</u> feel nervous. It's hard for ____me_____.

3. Some <u>people</u> speak very fast. I can't understand ____them_____.

4. My sister hates <u>spiders</u>, but I'm not afraid of _____them____.

5. I have a <u>test</u> coming up. I'm not worried about _____it_____.

6. <u>We</u> are studying English. It can help _____us_____ get jobs.

7. <u>Maria</u> is my best friend. I text _____her_____ every day.

8. Can <u>you</u> speak Italian? I can teach _____you_____ some words.

D Which sentences in **C** are true for you? In your notebook, rewrite the ones that are not true for you so that they are.

E Work with a partner. Take turns saying your sentences from **D**. Your partner can ask questions.

> " I speak English at school. I speak it outside class, too.
>
> Really? Where? "

> " I use it at work. How about you?
>
> I don't use it outside class often. "

ACTIVE ENGLISH Try it out!

A WRITING Look at the gameboard in **B**. In your notebook, answer the questions in the white squares. Turn to the Writing appendix to see an example.

B Play the game with a partner.

1. Student A goes first. Flip a coin (Heads = move one space; Tails = move two spaces).

2. When you land on a square, complete the task. If you do it correctly, you get one or two points (see box).

3. Play until you reach the "FINISH" square. The person with the most points wins.

Gray Squares
One point for a correct answer
White Squares
Two points for using correct grammar and vocabulary

START	1. Act out the sentence: *I'm tired.*	2. Some people are afraid of dogs. Are you afraid of them? Explain.	3. Your friend has a job interview today. Complete the expression: *Good _____!*
7. Your friend is sad because her dog is sick. Complete the expression. _____ *there!*	6. When you speak English, how do you feel? Why?	5. You see a man smiling and laughing. He probably feels _____.	4. Name a sad song. Do you like it or not?
8. On the weekend, how do you usually feel? Why?	9. Complete the conversation. **A:** *How are you?* **B:** *I'm _____. How _____?*	10. When you talk in front of the class, is it hard for you? Why?	11. Act out the sentence: *I'm bored.*
FINISH Act out the sentence: *I'm so excited!*	14. How do you feel right now? Why?	13. Someone is shouting in class. Complete the expression: *C_____ d_____!*	12. Imagine you can't find your phone. How do you feel? Why?

2B GOALS Now I can . . .

Explain how I feel _____

Talk about things I am afraid of _____

1. Yes, I can.
2. Mostly, yes.
3. Not yet.

GLOBAL VOICES

A You are going to watch people talking about their feelings. How do they feel about each activity? Guess. Put the activities into the categories.

dancing	getting on an airplane	planning a vacation	shopping alone	trying new food
eating	going to the beach	reading the news	traveling	watching soccer

Happy	Excited	Sad	Relaxed	Bored

B Watch the video. Check your answers in **A**. How many are correct?

C Watch the video again. Choose **T** for *true* and **F** for *false*.

1. Alexandra says dancing helps her to stay healthy.   **T**   **F**
2. Chiyuki likes finding excellent restaurants.   **T**   **F**
3. Alexandra loves to travel with her friends.   **T**   **F**
4. Chiyuki doesn't like to fly.   **T**   **F**
5. Daniele's favorite sport is soccer.   **T**   **F**

D Complete the sentences so that they are true for you.

1. I'm happy when I'm _____.
2. I'm excited when I'm _____.
3. I'm sad when I'm _____.
4. I'm relaxed when I'm _____.
5. I'm bored when I'm _____.

E Work with a partner. Take turns telling each other your sentences from **D**.

People dance at a silent disco in Edinburgh, Scotland. How do you feel when you're dancing?

3

SHOPPING

LOOK AT THE PHOTO. ANSWER THE QUESTIONS.

1. What are the people doing?

2. What is a similar place where you live?

WARM-UP VIDEO

A Work with a partner. Make a list of things you like and dislike about grocery shopping.

Grocery Shopping	
I like . . .	I dislike . . .

B Watch the video. What does the woman dislike about grocery shopping? Does she dislike the same things as you and your partner?

C Watch the video again. Use the words in the box to complete each sentence.

break drives looks makes takes waits

1. _____ The woman _____ in a long line of people.

2. _____ A man _____ the last box of cereal.

3. _____ The bags _____ when the woman arrives home.

4. _____ The woman _____ for a parking spot.

5. _____ The woman _____ a list.

6. _____ The woman _____ to the supermarket.

D Watch the video one more time. Put the sentences in **C** in the correct order.

Shoppers explore
Market Hall in
Rotterdam, Netherlands.

GOALS

Lesson A
/ Identify common foods
/ Talk about things you need

Lesson B
/ Describe shopping habits
/ Discuss different places to shop and what they sell

VOCABULARY

A Practice saying the food items in the picture. Which ones do you eat? Do you eat any of them every day? Tell a partner.

B Complete the chart with examples for each type of food. Use words from the picture and your own ideas.

Fresh Food	Frozen Food	Junk Food	Breakfast Food

C Work with a partner. Ask and answer questions about your foods in **B**.

1. What is one food in your chart that is not in the picture?
2. Which items in your chart do you like? Are there any items you don't like?

LISTENING

A Practice saying the words aloud. Then listen and repeat. 🎧17

    1. fish   **2.** soda   **3.** potato

B PRONUNCIATION: Syllables Work with a partner. Read each word aloud. How many syllables does it have: one, two, or three? Guess. Then listen and check your answers. 🎧18

	1	2	3
1. milk	☐	☐	☐
2. carrots	☐	☐	☐
3. tomato	☐	☐	☐
4. cheese	☐	☐	☐
5. banana	☐	☐	☐
6. cake	☐	☐	☐
7. yogurt	☐	☐	☐
8. apple	☐	☐	☐
9. cereal	☐	☐	☐
10. ice cream	☐	☐	☐

C Allison is going to the store. Listen. Choose the items that she and her mom talk about. 🎧19

bananas   ice cream
bread   lettuce
carrots   milk
chicken   potatoes

D Allison is at the store. Listen. Complete the sentence. 🎧20

Allison's mom doesn't want _____. She wants _____.

E How do Allison and her mom talk about the foods they need? Complete the sentences.

bunch   carton   head   loaf

    1. A _____ of bread.
    2. A _____ of lettuce.
    3. A _____ of ice cream.
    4. A _____ of carrots.

F Work with a partner. Make a list of the foods Allison is buying. What do you think her mom is cooking?

SPEAKING

A Read the conversation and listen. Underline the foods Rachel and Ken have. Circle the food they need. Then answer the questions. 🎧21

Rachel: Let's check our shopping list. What do we have?

Ken: Well, we have a cake, two cartons of ice cream, and 21 candles.

Rachel: That's great! I love surprise parties. I hope Susanna likes cake.

Ken: She does. It's her favorite.

Rachel: Good. What else do we need?

Ken: Well, there are 12 people coming to the party. We still need some snacks. Let's get some chips.

Rachel: OK. The party is on Friday. Today is Tuesday. We have some time.

Ken: Is that everything? Do we need anything else?

Rachel: Hmmm . . . Let me think . . .

1. What kind of party is it? How do you know?
2. How many people are attending the party?
3. When is the party?

Many people around the world celebrate a birthday with cake.

B Practice the conversation in **A** with a partner.

C Work with a different partner. Imagine you are planning a birthday party for your friend. Make a list of things you need.

Food	Snacks	Drinks	Other
birthday cake	popcorn	juice	balloons

SPEAKING STRATEGY 🎧22
Talking about Things You Need

What do we have?	We have coffee and donuts.
What else do we need?	We still need plates and napkins. Nothing. We have everything.
Do we need anything else?	Yes, we (still) need cream and sugar. No, that's it. We have everything.
Use *still* for unfinished actions. It comes before the verb.	

D With your partner, make your own conversation. Use your information in **C** to talk about things you need for your party.

E Take turns. Perform your conversation for another pair of students. Does the other party sound fun? What do you like about it?

" What drinks do we have?

We have juice. We still need to get some soda. "

" Got it. Do we need anything else?

GRAMMAR

A Read the Unit 3, Lesson A Grammar Reference in the appendix. Complete the exercises. Then do the exercises below.

COUNT AND NONCOUNT NOUNS	
Count	**Noncount**
a tomato, an apple, two carrots, three eggs	bread, rice, coffee, sugar

B Study the chart in **A**. With a partner, complete each sentence with *count nouns* or *noncount nouns*.

1. _____ can follow *a* or *an*.

2. _____ can follow numbers.

3. _____ are always singular.

4. _____ have singular and plural forms.

C Complete the sentences with *a* or *an*. If nothing is needed, leave the space blank.

1. Do you want _____ rice or _____ baked potato with your dinner?

2. My uncle likes to have _____ fruit for breakfast. He usually eats _____ apple or _____ banana.

3. _____ tea tastes good without _____ sugar.

4. I often eat _____ chips as a snack.

5. Is there _____ salt in this soup?

6. I have _____ cereal and _____ egg every morning.

D Read the sentences. Choose **T** for *true* or **F** for *false* to give your own answers.

1. I don't like soda because it has too much sugar.   **T**   **F**

2. I usually eat pasta once or twice a week.   **T**   **F**

3. You can usually find apples, oranges, or some kind of fruit in my refrigerator.   **T**   **F**

4. I eat more bread than rice.   **T**   **F**

5. I drink at least two glasses of water a day.   **T**   **F**

6. I need coffee in the morning to wake up.   **T**   **F**

7. I don't eat hot soup in the summer.   **T**   **F**

8. I eat too much candy.   **T**   **F**

E Work with a partner. Discuss your answers in **D**. Then decide which food and drink items are count nouns and which are noncount nouns.

66 Soda has too much sugar, but I like it.

Me, too. I drink a can of soda every day. 99

Banh mi sandwiches
are from Vietnam.

A Read the list of ingredients for each dish. Look up any new words in a dictionary.

Lamb Curry and Rice			Corn and Tomato Soup		
lamb	curry powder	rice	tomatoes	garlic	corn
onions	yogurt		soup broth	pepper	
Banh Mi Sandwich			Creamy Mashed Potatoes		
bread	cucumber	carrots	potatoes	green onions	butter
chicken	mayonnaise		salt	cream cheese	

B Work in a group of four students. Each student chooses a different dish in **A**. Complete the task.

1. On five small pieces of paper, write each ingredient from your recipe.

2. Give the five pieces of paper to your teacher.

3. Your teacher will mix all the papers for your group. Take the five papers your teacher gives you.

C Look at the five pieces of paper from your teacher. Which ingredients do you have for your recipe? Which ones do you need? Make a list.

D Move around the classroom. Talk to your classmates to find the ingredients for your dish. Sit down when you get all five.

> 66 I'm making corn and tomato soup.
> I need some tomatoes.

> Sorry, I don't have tomatoes.
> Do you need anything else? 99

> 66 I also need garlic.

> Oh, I have garlic.
> Here you go. 99

Seated Players: Other students can still ask you questions. You can give them your extra ingredients.

Standing Players: Find your ingredients quickly. You don't want to be the last person standing!

3A GOALS   Now I can . . .

Identify common foods _____

Talk about things I need _____

1. Yes, I can.

2. Mostly, yes.

3. Not yet.

VOCABULARY

A Look at the verbs in the box. How many do you know? Look up any new words in a dictionary.

buy	pay	sell	try on
go shopping	return	spend	

WORD BANK
You **pay** <u>for</u> an item.
You **pay** <u>with</u> a credit card.
You **spend** money <u>on</u> an item.

B Complete the sentences with the words from **A**. Then check your answers with a partner.

1. ☐ I _____try on_____ shoes or clothes before I buy them.
2. ☐ I sometimes _____sell_____ old comics to make money.
3. ☐ I find things on sale. I don't ___pay spend___ full price for anything.
4. ☐ I ___spend pay___ a lot of money on coffee every week.
5. ☐ I like to ___go shopping___ with my friends.
6. ☐ Sometimes, I _____buy_____ clothes or shoes online.
7. ☐ When clothes don't fit, I ___return___ them and get my money back.

C Think about your shopping habits. Check (✓) the sentences in **B** that are true for you.

D Work with a partner. Ask and answer questions about the information in **B**.

❝ Do you try on shoes before you buy them?

Yes, I do. I don't want to go back to the store. ❞

Stores get very busy around the holidays.

$25 DEALS!

$25 DEALS!

$25

A MAGICAL MARKET

A Do you know any famous markets? What can you buy there? Tell a partner.

B Scan the article. Write three things that people can buy at this famous market.

_____

_____

C **Check comprehension.** Read the article. Choose **T** for *true* and **F** for *false*. Rewrite the false sentences in your notebook to make them true.

1. The market is new.   **T**   **F**

2. The market is only popular with local people.   **T**   **F**

3. The shops are only on the main street.   **T**   **F**

GLOBAL VOICES

A Choose the sentence with a similar meaning.

This is my local market.

1. This is a market I really like.
2. This is a market that is close to my home.
3. This is an outdoor market.

WORD BANK
At a market, a **stall** is where people can buy things.

B Watch the video. Check (✓) the food that Jan does not mention.

☐ fish   ☐ meat   ☐ rice   ☐ bread

C Match the speaker with their favorite stall. Then watch the video again and check your answers.

Jan	the cheese stall
Amy	the fruit and vegetable stall
Richard	the fish stall

D Complete the sentences with the words from the box.

bones	fish	meat	tomatoes

1. Jan dislikes _____ because it has _____.
2. Amy dislikes _____.
3. Richard dislikes _____.

E Think about your local market or supermarket. Make a list of what you can buy there. Is there anything special about it? Then tell a partner.

" At my local supermarket, you can buy live lobsters.

That's cool, but I don't like seafood. "

The Oxford Covered Market in Oxford, UK

A lot of men are growing beards.

A Read the information. Then look at the trends. Are they popular in your country? Why or why not? Tell a partner.

> A *trend* is a popular activity. Many people are doing it at the same time. New trends in food, shopping, and personal appearance are happening all the time.

Food and Drink More people are eating less meat these days.

_____

_____

Shopping Many young people are buying and selling used clothes online.

_____

_____

Appearance A lot of men are growing beards.

_____

_____

B Work with a partner. Add some trends to the lists in **A**. Write sentences using the present continuous and the language in the box.

Talking about Trends
• Everyone is . . .
• Many people are . . .
• A lot of women / men are . . .
• People in their twenties are . . .
• More young people are . . .

C You and your partner are going to talk about a trend. Choose <u>one</u> of your ideas in **A**. Why is the trend popular?

D You and your partner are going to interview three people each about your trend. For each interview, follow these steps:

1. Greet the person. Ask how they are.

2. Ask the person for some basic information (name, age, job, city). Write it in the chart.

3. Tell the person about your trend.

4. Ask for the person's opinion of the trend. Write their response in the chart.

Name	Age	Job	City	Opinion of the Trend

66 | These days, a lot of people are . . .
Do you like this trend? Why or why not?

E After your interviews, compare your information with your partner's. Then answer the questions.

1. Do a lot of people like the trend or not?

2. Do people of different ages have different opinions?

F **You Choose** Choose an option to present your information with your partner.

Option 1 Write a social media post of 70–100 words.

Option 2 Make a short video presentation.

Option 3 Create a photo collage.

In your project, answer the following questions:

1. What is the trend?

2. Why is it popular?

3. What do people think of it? Use quotes from people you interviewed.

G Work with another pair of students. Complete the task. Then change roles and repeat.

1. **Pair 1:** Present your trend.

2. **Pair 2:** Listen. Tell Pair 1 how you feel about their trend.

A small village in the desert of southwestern Peru is a popular place for tourists.

GOALS

Lesson A
/ Talk about the weather
/ Give and respond to advice

Lesson B
/ Say who owns something
/ Plan for a trip

VACATION

LOOK AT THE PHOTO. ANSWER THE QUESTIONS.

1. Where are the people? How's the weather?
2. What is a popular place for vacation in your country? Why is it popular?

WARM-UP VIDEO

A The video shows friends on a road trip* in the US. They visit four states. Say them with your teacher. Circle the places you know.

_____ Arizona
_____ California
_____ New Mexico
_____ Utah

* A **road trip** is a long-distance trip by car.

B Watch the video. Number the states in **A** in the order the friends visit each one.

C What do the friends see on their road trip? Watch the video again and choose the correct answers.

1. a beautiful night sky
2. animals
3. beaches
4. beautiful red rocks
5. large cactus
6. mountains
7. old houses
8. the ocean

D Answer the questions with a partner.

1. Do you like this road trip? Why or why not?
2. At the end of the video, the woman asks, "Where do you want to go?" What is your answer?

VOCABULARY

A Say the sentences in the Word Bank with the class.

B Look at the weather report for three cities. Complete the sentences.

TORONTO
-3°C / 26°F

TOKYO
13°C / 55°F

HAVANA
23°C / 73°F

WORD BANK

	cloudy.	
	sunny.	
It's	windy.	
	raining.	
	snowing.	
	hot.	
	warm.	
	comfortable.	
It's	chilly / cool.	
	cold.	
	freezing.	

Toronto

1. It's **raining / snowing**.

2. It's _____ degrees. It's **chilly / freezing**.

Tokyo

3. It's **sunny / cloudy** and **cool / warm**.

4. It's _____ degrees.

Havana

5. It's **windy / sunny** and **warm / hot**.

6. It's _____ degrees.

C Work with a partner. Ask about the weather in each city in **B**. Then cover your answers and ask again.

❝ How's the weather in Tokyo?
      It's . . . ❞

D With your partner, find the weather in your area and two other places anywhere in the world.

E Tell a new partner about the weather for your places in **D**. Which place has the best weather?

LISTENING

A **Make predictions.** Read the two questions. Can you guess any answers?

1. When is a good time to visit?
   a. Toronto: _____ freezing Jun _____ and _____ July _____
   b. Tokyo: _____ July _____ or _____ Aug _____
   c. Havana: _____ and _____

2. How's the weather?

   a. Toronto

   b. Tokyo

   c. Havana

B Listen. Answer the first question in **A**. Write the months. 🎧25

C Listen. Answer the second question in **A**. Match the cities and the weather. 🎧26

D Listen again. Write **T** for *true* or **F** for *false*. If a sentence is false, correct it in your notebook. 🎧26

Toronto	**Tokyo**	**Havana**
1. It's hot both months. _____	3. It's warm at that time of year. _____	5. Early in the year, it's 85 degrees during the day. _____
2. It rains sometimes. _____	4. It's usually six degrees in the afternoon. _____	6. It's the rainy season. _____

E Choose one city from the podcast. Then work with a partner to ask and answer the questions.

1. When is a good time to visit? How is the weather?

2. When you go there, what is something you should take? Think about the weather and things to do.

" A good time to visit Tokyo is . . .

Some people find interesting ways to view the cherry blossoms in Tokyo, Japan.

In some parts of Costa Rica, visitors can explore the mountains and relax on the beach on the same day.

SPEAKING

A Read the conversation and listen. How is the weather in Costa Rica? 🎧27

Rosa: Are you ready for your trip to Costa Rica?

Nick: Yeah. See? I have T-shirts, shorts, sandals, sunscreen . . .

Rosa: Where are you going exactly?

Nick: The beach *and* the mountains. All over, really.

Rosa: Hmm . . . you know, it's warm at the beach, but in the mountains, it can be cool.

Nick: Really?

Rosa: Yeah, so you should take a sweater or a jacket.

Nick: Good idea. Anything else?

Rosa: It rains sometimes, so you should also take a raincoat.

Nick: OK, I will. Thanks for telling me!

B Practice the conversation in **A** with a partner.

C What advice does Rosa give Nick? How does he reply? Underline the sentences in the conversation.

D Work with a partner. Choose a situation (1 or 2). Create a short role play. Use the Speaking Strategy.

Student A: Give advice to your partner in two different ways.

Student B: Refuse your partner's advice the first time. Then accept it.

1. You're at the beach. It's hot and sunny. Your partner wants to go swimming but sunburns easily.

2. Your partner wants to drive to a popular tourist site, but it's raining, and the road isn't safe.

SPEAKING STRATEGY 🎧28
Giving and Responding to Advice

Giving Advice	Accepting	Refusing
You should take a jacket.	Good idea. OK, I will.	(Thanks, but) I'll be OK.
I don't think you should wear shorts. You shouldn't wear shorts.	Yeah, you're right.	Don't worry. (I'll be OK.)

E Change roles and repeat the task in **D**. Use the other situation.

GRAMMAR

A Read the Unit 4, Lesson A Grammar Reference in the appendix. Complete the exercises. Then do the exercises below.

CONNECTING IDEAS WITH *BUT*, *OR*, AND *SO*
It's sunny **but** cool today.   It's a nice day **but** a little chilly.   It's warm in the afternoon, **but** it's cold at night.
Let's visit Montreal in June **or** July.   We can stay with my family **or** with friends.   We can walk to the festival, **or** we can ride our bikes.
It's chilly, **so** you should take a jacket.

i Using Commas

Notice that you use a comma to separate clauses with *but*, *or*, and *so*.

B Complete the sentences with your own ideas.

1. It's raining, so _____.

2. It's a nice day outside, but _____.

3. You can drive or _____ to the airport.

4. It's warm, so _____.

5. I want to visit Paris, but _____.

6. You can pay with cash or _____.

7. I like to travel, but _____.

8. It's summer vacation, so _____.

9. Is it hot there in August or _____?

10. I want to improve my English, so _____.

11. It's chilly in Toronto, but _____.

12. She wants to visit Mexico or _____.

C Work with a partner. Look at your sentences in **B**. Does each one show a contrast (a difference), give choices, or introduce a result?

D Work with a new partner. Follow the steps to play the game.

1. Write the numbers *1–12* on small pieces of paper.

2. Mix the numbers and put them in a pile face down on the desk.

3. Read the directions to play the game.

1. **Student A:** Choose a number.* Find it on the list (1–12) in **B**.
2. Make a sentence.
   - **Correct sentence:** Check (✓) the number on your score card.
   - **Incorrect sentence:** Leave the number on your score card blank.

Note: You *cannot* repeat your partner's correct answer.

3. Put the piece of paper at the bottom of the pile.
4. Then it is **Student B**'s turn. Repeat steps 1–3.

To win: Be the first person to check 1–12 on your score card.

Score Card			
1	☐	7	☐
2	☐	8	☐
3	☐	9	☐
4	☐	10	☐
5	☐	11	☐
6	☐	12	☐

*If you chose this number and answered correctly already, put it back in the pile.

Ziplining is a popular activity in Chiang Mai, Thailand.

ACTIVE ENGLISH Try it out!

A   A student is introducing you to their city. Complete the sentences with *but*, *or*, or *so*.

Visitor's Guide: Chiang Mai, Thailand

How's the weather?
Chiang Mai has three seasons: hot, cool, and rainy, (1.) _____ the weather is usually warm all year.

When is a good time to visit?
The cool season is from November to February. It's sunny and warm, (2.) _____ it's the perfect time to visit. In April, it's very hot. In May, the rainy season starts.

What should I bring?
You should bring clothes for warm and cool weather. From November to February, it's warm during the day, (3.) _____ at night, it's chilly sometimes.

What can I do in Chiang Mai?
You should take a Thai cooking class (4.) _____ go ziplining in the rainforest outside the city!

B   Work with a partner. Ask and answer the questions in the visitor's guide.

C   With your partner, make a visitor's guide to introduce a town or city you know. Answer the four questions with your own ideas.

D   Work with another pair of students. Show them your visitor's guide and explain it using photos or video.

4A GOALS	Now I can . . .	
Talk about the weather _____		1. Yes, I can.
Give and respond to advice _____		2. Mostly, yes.
		3. Not yet.

VOCABULARY

A Match the verbs and nouns. Use some words more than once.

buy — photos

go — a suitcase

pack — sightseeing

take — a ticket

— a trip

B **PRONUNCIATION: Sentence Stress** Listen to the three sentences. Notice the stress of the underlined words. Then listen again and repeat. 🎧29

1. Let's <u>go sightseeing</u> this afternoon.

2. Do you <u>go shopping</u> when you visit a city?

3. I like to <u>go swimming</u> on summer vacation.

C Work with a partner. Answer the questions.

1. Do you have a suitcase? What color is it?

2. What do you pack for cold weather?

3. What do you pack for hot weather?

4. On a trip, what do you take photos of?

5. Where do you want to take a trip?

6. Look at the photo. What is another good place to go sightseeing?

Tourists "hold up" the leaning Tower of Pisa in Italy.

GETTING READY!

Packing tips for your next trip

To explore the ice caves in Iceland, people need to wear warm clothes.

Imagine this: You're taking a trip to a faraway[1] place, like South Africa or Iceland. You're so excited—you just want to get on the plane and go! But first, you need to pack your suitcase.

Taking a trip is fun, but packing usually is not. "What should I bring?" travelers often ask. Many people are unsure and pack too much. How can you pack your things in one easy-to-carry bag? Here are some helpful tips for your next trip:

1. _____. You only *need* a few things on your trip: your passport, credit cards, cell phone, and certain clothes (a suit for work, a sweater for cool weather, shorts for hot weather). What do you really need? Make a list. Then pack only those important things.

2. _____. Do you plan to read on the trip? Leave books at home. They're heavy.[2] If you want to read, bring a tablet, or buy magazines or books at the airport. When you're done, you can leave them on the plane or at your hotel.

3. _____. Bring mostly white, black, gray, tan,[3] and blue clothes and shoes. These colors are easy to mix and match.[4] By doing this, you can pack less.

4. _____. Are you taking a trip to a chilly place like Iceland? If so, wear some of your warm clothes—like sweaters, jackets, or boots—on the plane instead of putting them in your suitcase. These things take up a lot of room in your suitcase and make it heavy.

5. _____. Use them to organize[5] the items in your suitcase. Put things like your toothbrush, soap, and shampoo in one bag; underwear and socks in a second bag; shirts in a third one; and so on. This way, you use less space in your suitcase; it's also easy to unpack! 🎧30

[1] A **faraway** place is not nearby.
[2] A **heavy** object weighs a lot.
[3] **Tan** is a light brown color.
[4] When you **mix and match** a group of things, you put them together so they look good.
[5] When you **organize** things, you put them together in a neat way.

A Answer the questions with a partner.

1. How long does it take you to pack for a trip? Do you like to pack? Why or why not?

2. Read the title of the article. What is one tip in the article? Guess.

B **Identify topic sentences.** Read the article. Write each tip in the correct paragraph.

Don't bring books	Make a list	Wear your warm clothes on the plane
Choose simple colors	Use small bags	

C Answer the questions according to the article.

1. What should you write on your list?

2. Why should you bring a tablet?

3. Which colors are best to pack? Why?

4. Why should you wear warm clothes on the plane?

5. How are small bags helpful?

D Ask and answer the questions in **C** with a partner.

E In your opinion, which tip is the best? Can you think of any other tips? Tell your partner.

LISTENING

A Listen to three short conversations. Choose the sentence that best describes each one. 🎧31

Conversation 1

Sentence 1   Sentence 2   Sentence 3   Sentence 4

Conversation 2

Sentence 1   Sentence 2   Sentence 3   Sentence 4

Conversation 3

Sentence 1   Sentence 2   Sentence 3   Sentence 4

B Listen. Complete the sentences. Then listen again and check your answers. 🎧32

1. **A:** Here it is: Row 28, Seat C. Oh . . . _____ me.

   B: Yes?

   A: I think you're _____ in my seat.

2. **A:** Excuse me, whose backpack is this? This _____ one—is it yours?

   B: No, it's not mine.

   C: Oh, it _____ to me.

3. **A:** May I see your _____, please?

   B: Sure. Here you go.

   A: Are you visiting for _____ or for pleasure?

> 66 I think you're
> sitting in my seat.
>
>   I don't
>   think so. 99

C Work with a partner. Choose a conversation in **B**. Add 2–3 sentences to it and practice your conversation.

> 66 Look at my
> ticket. I have the
> window seat.
>
>   Oh, you're right.
>   I'm sorry. 99

D Perform your conversation for another pair of students.

People get ready for a flight.

GRAMMAR

A Read the Unit 4, Lesson B Grammar Reference in the appendix. Complete the exercises. Then do the exercises below.

	POSSESSIVE ADJECTIVES	WHOSE	POSSESSIVE PRONOUNS
I have a passport.	**My** passport is green.	**Whose** passport is this?	It's **mine**.
You have a passport.	**Your** passport is green.		It's **yours**.
She has a passport	**Her** passport is green.		It's **hers**.
He has a passport.	**His** passport is green.		It's **his**.
We have tickets.	**Our** tickets are free.	**Whose** tickets are these?	They're **ours**.
They have tickets.	**Their** tickets are free.		They're **theirs**.

B Look at the chart in **A**. Choose the correct answers.

1. Words like *my*, *your*, and *her* **go before** / **follow** nouns.

2. Words like *mine*, *yours*, and *hers* **go before** / **follow** the verb *be*.

3. What do you notice about the word *his*?

C Work in groups of four. Follow the steps to play the game.

Round 1 | Do the following:

1. **Student A:** Close your eyes.

2. **Students B–D:** Write your favorite place for a day trip on a small piece of paper. For example: *the beach* or *the mountains*.

3. Put all the papers face up on the desk. **Student A:** Open your eyes.

4. **Student B:** Point to one of the papers. Ask **Student A:** *Whose answer is this?*

5. **Student A:** Try to guess the writer. Say three sentences for each paper:

" I think this answer is yours / his / hers.

It belongs to you / her / him. "

" The beach is your / her / his favorite place.

6. Keep guessing until there are no more papers. Score one point for each correct guess.

Play three more rounds | Each person should be Student A for one round. Choose a different topic from the box each time. The player with the most points wins.

> Your favorite . . .
> **Round 1** Place for a day trip
> **Round 2** Movie
> **Round 3** Drink
> **Round 4** Singer

ACTIVE ENGLISH Try it out!

A Read Sofia and Angelo's ad. Then answer the questions with a partner.

Lovely Apartment with Balcony

2 guests | 2 beds | 1 bath   Hosted by Sofia and Angelo

Great location—perfect for tourists
Beautiful ocean view | Close to restaurants

1. Who are Sofia and Angelo?
2. How many people can stay in this apartment?
3. What are two things you like about this apartment?

B Choose the correct answers to complete the notes from Sofia and Angelo.

Your apartment is upstairs. The downstairs apartment belongs to (1.) **ours / us**.

The apartment has (2.) **it's / its** own kitchen.

You can enjoy (3.) **you / your** morning coffee on the balcony.

Sofia has a password for the wifi. You can use (4.) **her / hers**.

You can rent a bicycle or use one of (5.) **our / ours**.

(6.) **Your / Yours** check-in time is any time after 3:00 p.m.

(7.) **Our / Ours** city is sunny and warm in July. It's very hilly.

> **i** *It's* and *Its*
> *it's = it is*
> *my / your / its*

C Plan a trip to stay in Sofia and Angelo's apartment in July. What should you pack? Make a list and compare it with a partner's. How are your lists the same? How are they different?

D **WRITING** You need to send an email to your hosts, Sofia and Angelo. Turn to the Writing appendix to see an example. What are the writer's questions? What is Angelo's answer?

E Read the situation. You have a question for your hosts. Write an informal email to them.

> You and your friend are arriving at 10:00 a.m. You want to join a sightseeing tour at 11:00 a.m. You are each traveling with a large suitcase. Check-in time is after 3:00 p.m.

4B GOALS   Now I can . . .

Say who owns something ____	1. Yes, I can.
Plan for a trip ____	2. Mostly, yes.
	3. Not yet.

GLOBAL VOICES

A Watch the video. Write the item each speaker talks about.

| camera | DVDs | GPS | hat | headlamp | lucky bracelet | medicine | sunscreen |

1. Carlton Ward _____
2. Amy Dickman _____
3. Eric Patterson _____
4. Lee Berger _____
5. Chris Thornton _____
6. Kuenga Wangmo _____
7. Alizé Carrère _____
8. Cory Richards _____

B Why does each speaker in **A** take that item? Read the sentences. Then watch the video and write the missing words.

1. Without a GPS, we would be still paddling in _____ somewhere.
2. DVDs . . . [It] just gives me something to _____ at that's nothing to do with the field . . .
3. . . . the _____ goes out. A headlamp has become sort of an essential tool . . .
4. It's my _____ hat. I make my discoveries with my hat on.
5. a mini pharmacy . . . I always get _____ when I travel.
6. a camera . . . a way to _____ that which I am experiencing.

C What do you always travel with? Why? Make notes in your notebook.

D Work in a small group. Share your answer to the question in **C**. Don't read your notes. Are any of your answers the same?

> 66 In the summer, I usually go to the beach with my friends. It's hot and sunny there, so I always pack sunscreen and my sunglasses.

What item do you think Lee Berger never leaves home without?

Images of firefighters are projected onto the Sydney Opera House, Australia.

GOALS

Lesson A
/ Talk about interesting people
/ Agree or disagree with an opinion

Lesson B
/ Narrate a story
/ Describe actions and people you admire

5

HEROES

LOOK AT THE PHOTO. ANSWER THE QUESTIONS.

1. What job do the people on the building do? Why are they on the building?
2. Look up the word *hero* in a dictionary. What words describe a hero?

WARM-UP VIDEO

A Work with a partner. Look up the words in a dictionary and write a definition for each one.

emergency

_____

rescue

_____

volunteer

_____

B Look at your definitions in **A**. What do you think the video is about?

C Watch the video. Choose the correct answers according to what you hear. All sentences have more than one answer.

1. People _____ the ocean.
   a. work on   b. live next to   c. visit
2. The water is _____.
   a. dangerous b. cold   c. deep
3. The volunteers are _____.
   a. teachers   b. students   c. doctors
4. Sometimes, the volunteers are at _____ when an emergency happens.
   a. work   b. school   c. family events
5. Iona learned to be _____.
   a. afraid b. helpful   c. a strong swimmer

D Tell a partner about the volunteers from the video. Use your own words.

VOCABULARY

A Look at the photo and read the caption. What is Idabel? Tell a partner.

B Read about Erika Bergman. Tell a partner two things she does. Which activities are interesting to you? Why?

Erika Bergman is an **explorer**.	She's a deep-sea submarine* **pilot**. She uses submarines, like Idabel, to go to exciting new places.
She's a **traveler**.	She visits different countries to learn about underwater life around the world.
She's a **speaker**.	She shares stories about her trips under the ocean with students and other people.
She's a **scientist** with a love of machines.	She has experience working on big ships and submarines.
She's a **teacher**.	Her camp teaches girls to build underwater robots.

*A **submarine** is a ship that travels underwater.

C Read the words in the box. Then complete the task.

educator	presenter	researcher

1. The words **author** and **writer** have similar meanings. Can you find words in **B** with similar meanings to the words in the box?

2. Use two of the words in **blue** to tell a partner about a famous person you know.

**Erika Bergman
with Idabel**

A seal swims under the sea ice in Antarctica.

LISTENING

A Say the words in the box. Then listen and repeat. Notice the stress. 🎧33

> photo   photographer   photography

B Listen to the interview. Choose the words that describe Alex. 🎧34

explorer   photographer   scientist   tourist   traveler   writer

C Listen again. Write the missing words to complete the questions only. 🎧34

1. **Q:** _____ _____ _____ there?   **A:** _____ very _____. It's also _____ and _____.

2. **Q:** _____ _____ there?   **A:** _____ from around the world.

3. **Q:** _____ _____ the scientists _____?   **A:** _____ of things.

4. **Q:** _____ _____ that _____?   **A:** We _____ a hole in the _____.

5. **Q:** _____ _____ for you, Alex?   **A:** I want to _____ a _____.

D Listen one more time. Complete Alex's answers. 🎧34

E **Identify sequences.** Alex takes photos of animals under the sea ice. How does he do it? Listen to part of the interview. Then tell a partner the steps. 🎧35

F Do you think people living and working in Antarctica are heroes? Why or why not? Tell your partner.

SPEAKING

A Read the conversation and listen. Then complete the task. 🎧36

Kurt: Hey, Maggie. What movie are you watching tonight?

Maggie: It's called *Hidden Figures*. It's a biopic. It's my second time watching it. Do you know it?

Kurt: *Hidden Figures*? Is that the one about the team of women mathematicians?

Maggie: Yes, that's it. It's a great movie.

Kurt: I agree. I think the story is exciting. What do you like about it?

Maggie: The three women.

Kurt: Me, too! They were really brave.

Maggie: Hey, do you want to watch the movie with me?

Kurt: Again? Well . . . sure. Why not?

1. Find a word that means "a movie that tells a person's story."

2. Find a word that means "not afraid."

3. Do Kurt and Maggie like the movie? How do you know?

Mathematician Mary Winston Jackson (1921–2005) was the first African American female engineer to work at NASA. She is one of the women featured in the movie *Hidden Figures*.

B Practice the conversation in **A** with a partner.

C Copy the chart into your notebook. Complete it with information about two movies you like.

Name of Movie	Actor(s) in Movie	Words to Describe Movie

SPEAKING STRATEGY 🎧37
Agreeing and Disagreeing with an Opinion

Statement: I think *Hidden Figures* is a good movie.		Follow-up questions
Agreeing	I think so, too. I agree.	What do you like about it?
Disagreeing	Really? I don't think so. Sorry, but I disagree.	Why do you say that?
You can agree with a negative statement by saying *me neither*. **A:** I don't like that movie. **B:** Me neither.		

D Work in a group. Talk about your movies. Use the information in **C** and the Speaking Strategy.

❝ I think *Frozen 2* is a good movie.

Really? I don't think so. ❞

❝ Why do you say that?

GRAMMAR

A Read the Unit 5, Lesson A Grammar Reference in the appendix. Complete the exercises. Then do the exercises below.

THE SIMPLE PAST WITH *BE*						
Affirmative and Negative Statements			**Yes / No Questions**			**Answers**
Subject	*Was / Were*		*Was / Were*	Subject		
I / He / She	**was** / wasn't	a scientist.	**Were**	you	a scientist?	Yes, I **was**. / No, I **wasn't**.
We / You / They	**were** / weren't	scientists.	**Was**	she		Yes, she **was**. / No, she wasn't.
Past forms of *be*: *am, is → was; am not, isn't → wasn't; are → were; aren't → weren't*						

Wh- Questions				**Answers**
Wh- word	*Was / Were*	Subject		
When	**was**	he	in Antarctica?	**Last** year. / A year **ago**. / **In** 2020.

B Read about Katherine Johnson. Complete the sentences with simple past forms of *be*.

In the 1960s, Katherine Johnson (1.) _____ a mathematician who worked for NASA—the United States' space program. At that time, it (2.) _____ common for a woman to do that job. Also at that time, there (3.) _____ many African American female mathematicians working for NASA. NASA (4.) _____ trying to send people into space, and along with Mary Winston Jackson and Dorothy Vaughan, Katherine (5.) _____ part of a team that helped NASA succeed. These three women (6.) _____ real pioneers! Many other Black female mathematicians and engineers (7.) _____ inspired by them, and the movie *Hidden Figures* (8.) _____ about their lives.

C Work with a partner. Take turns asking questions about Katherine Johnson's life.

❝ Was Katherine Johnson a mathematician?

Yes, she was. ❞

Mathematician Katherine Johnson (1918–2020) helped the United States send astronauts into space.

ACTIVE ENGLISH Try it out!

A Read the headings. Then think of famous people you know from the past and complete the chart.

Entertainers*	
Leaders	
Authors	
Teachers	
Scientists	
Other	

* **Entertainers** are singers, actors, musicians, and other performers.

Junko Tabei was the first woman to climb the highest mountain on every continent.

B Complete the task.

1. Imagine that you can meet four famous people from the past. Who do you want to meet? Choose four people from your list in **A**.

2. Complete the chart with information about the four people.

Name	What was their job?	What were they famous for?

C Work in groups of three. Compare your answers in **B**. Explain your choices. Together, agree on one list of four people to meet.

❝ Junko Tabei was a Japanese climber, author, and teacher. She was the first woman to reach the top of the highest mountains in places like Antarctica, Asia, Africa—all over the world!

She sounds interesting. ❞

5A GOALS Now I can . . .

Talk about interesting people _____

Agree or disagree with an opinion _____

1. Yes, I can.
2. Mostly, yes.
3. Not yet.

VOCABULARY

A How do you describe a kind person? Complete the sentences with the words in blue. Use a dictionary to look up new words.

admire	friendly	~~helpful~~	strangers	~~warm~~
caring	generous	selfish	together	

1. A **kind** person is _____helpful_____. They do nice things for others.

2. They are _____warm_____ and _____ with everybody. They say hello to friends, family members, and even _____.

3. They are _____. They give their time and money to help other people.

4. They are not _____. They think of others first.

5. Kind people often work in _____ jobs, like nursing and teaching.

6. Kind people bring other people _____.

7. Other people _____ kind people.

B Think of a kind person you admire. Write their name and your answers to the questions in your notebook.

1. How is the person helpful? Who do they help: family or strangers?

2. Is the person friendly? How do they show it?

3. When was the person generous?

C Work with a partner. Take turns asking the questions in **B**. Close your book when answering the questions.

An elephant keeper cares for a young elephant in Kenya.

PAY IT FORWARD

Picture this. You're in a cafe in Naples, Italy. A businessman enters and orders an espresso. He looks like he's in a hurry. He drinks his coffee quickly and before he leaves, he pays the bill. But strangely, he pays for not *one* coffee, but *two*. After the man leaves, the barista[1] writes the word *sospeso* on the receipt and hangs it in the window.

A sospeso or "suspended"[2] coffee is an Italian tradition of kindness. It started in Naples. It was popular during World War II. At that time, people wanted to help their neighbors.[3] After that, it became less popular. Recently though, more people are doing it again because of stories of kindness on the internet. There was also a popular movie called *Caffè Sospeso* or "Coffee for All."

When you buy a sospeso coffee, you pay for an extra cup of coffee so that a stranger can get one for free. Usually, a person with extra money pays for two coffees and leaves their receipt behind. Maybe the next customer is having a bad day, or they don't have much money. The free coffee tastes delicious and is helpful to them.

In the old part of Naples, Italy, Caffè Gambrinus serves about 1,000 sospeso coffees a year. Many of the coffee drinkers are older people.

This generous act doesn't happen only in Italy. People in other countries like Sweden and Brazil are also paying for two coffees and only drinking one. Why do people do it? Well, everyone likes to get a free coffee now and then. They feel good. And the person who buys the coffee feels good, too.

[1] A **barista** is a person who works in a coffee shop and prepares espresso drinks.
[2] When an action is **suspended**, you stop doing it and plan to do it later.
[3] **Neighbors** are people who live near each other.

A Work with a partner. Read the first paragraph of the article. Answer the questions.

1. What does the businessman do? What does the barista do?

2. What do you think happens next?

   a. The man returns to the cafe later and drinks the coffee.

   b. The man returns to the cafe later with a friend.

   c. Another person comes into the cafe and drinks the coffee.

B Read the rest of the article. How does a suspended coffee work? Complete the steps.

1. A person goes into a _____ and orders a _____.

2. The person drinks their _____.

3. The person only has _____ drink but pays for _____.

4. They leave their _____, and the barista puts it in the _____.

5. Later, another person enjoys a _____ drink.

C **Use existing knowledge.** Find the words in the article.

1. Find a word in Paragraph 1 that means "bill." _____

2. Find a word in Paragraph 2 that means "an old custom." _____

3. Find a word in Paragraph 4 that means "action." _____

D Work with a partner. Take turns asking and answering the questions.

1. How do people show generosity in cafes in Naples, Italy?

2. When was the tradition popular in the past? Why?

3. Why is it popular now?

4. Where else (outside Italy) can you find this act of kindness?

5. How is this tradition helpful?

E Discuss the questions with your partner.

1. What do you think of the tradition? Is there anything similar in your country?

2. Who do you want to buy a coffee for? Why?

LISTENING

A Read the sentence. What is a kind act you like to do? Tell a partner.

One small act of kindness can make someone else's day.

> " When I enter a building, I hold the door open.
>
> That's kind. Then the other person can go in first. "

B You are going to listen to a podcast. Read through the main points only and guess the missing information. Then listen and check your answers. 🎧39

Main Points	Examples
You don't need a lot of (1.) _____ to be generous.	Give a (5.) _____ to a friend.
You don't need to (2.) _____ for someone to ask for help.	Pick up trash in the (6.) _____.
You help your family and friends, but do you also help (3.) _____?	Help a (7.) _____ tourist.
You can be kind at (4.) _____, too.	Say (8.) _____ in the elevator.

C Listen again. Complete the examples. 🎧39

D Which acts of kindness in **B** do you want to try? Which ones do you not want to try? Why? Tell a partner.

> " I like the idea of sharing a book. It's nice to share things.
>
> I don't want to say hello to a stranger. I'm too shy! "

A woman looks at a book at a free library in Maine, US. At free libraries, people leave books for other people to take.

GRAMMAR

A Read the Unit 5, Lesson B Grammar Reference in the appendix. Complete the exercises. Then do the exercises below.

THE SIMPLE PAST: AFFIRMATIVE AND NEGATIVE STATEMENTS		
I / You / He / She / We / They	visit**ed**	Tokyo.
	didn't visit	
I / You / He / She / We / They	start**ed**	a company.
	didn't start	

Spelling Rules for Regular Verbs

move → move**d** study → stud**ied**

start → start**ed** stop → stop**ped**

B **PRONUNCIATION: Simple Past -ed Endings** Listen to the simple past forms. Say each word with the speaker. Pay attention to the pronunciation of the -ed ending. 🎧40

/t/	/d/	/ɪd/
liked, stopped	moved, tried	visited, waited

C How is the verb ending pronounced in each word? Listen and choose your answer. Then say the words with a partner. 🎧41

1. walked /t/ /ɪd/
2. started /d/ /ɪd/
3. wanted /d/ /ɪd/
4. returned /d/ /ɪd/
5. asked /t/ /ɪd/
6. cried /d/ /ɪd/
7. listened /d/ /ɪd/
8. needed /t/ /ɪd/
9. finished /t/ /ɪd/

D Work with a new partner. Complete Alec's story with simple past forms of the verbs. Then take turns reading the story aloud. Pay attention to the verb endings.

A few months ago, there was a girl named Alyssa in my class. I (1.) _____ (like) her a lot. One day, I (2.) _____ (invite) her to have dinner with me at a restaurant.

After dinner, I (3.) _____ (offer) to pay. I (4.) _____ (ask) the server for the check. I (5.) _____ (look) in my wallet, but I only had ten dollars. I (6.) _____ (need) 50 dollars. I (7.) _____ (not have) enough money!

I left the table. I (8.) _____ (try) to call my roommate from the bathroom, but he (9.) _____ (not answer) his phone. I left a message and (10.) _____ (explain) my problem.

Just then, the door (11.) _____ (open). It was my waiter. He (12.) _____ (hand) me 40 dollars. I (13.) _____ (promise) to pay him back, but he (14.) _____ (reply), "Don't worry about it." What a kind and generous guy!

E Ask and answer the questions about the story in **D** with your partner.

1. Where were Alec and Alyssa?
2. What happened after dinner?
3. When Alec realized his problem, what did he do?
4. Who helped Alec?
5. What did Alec promise?
6. How did the waiter reply?

ACTIVE ENGLISH Try it out!

A Read about Jason, Amanda, and Haruka. Who was the most helpful?

Jason, 30

Five years ago, Jason started his own company. Today, he is a very rich man. This year, he is paying for ten high school graduates to go to college.

Amanda, 16

A month ago, there was a car fire near Amanda's home. A little boy was in the car. Amanda pulled the child from the car and saved his life.

Haruka, 22

Haruka is in a wheelchair. This year, she climbed 3,776 meters (12,388 feet) to the top of Mount Fuji using special ropes. She's posting videos of her experience on social media.

B Work in groups of three. Complete the task.

1. Choose one of the people from **A**. Then close your book.
2. Explain your choice to the group.

> 66 I admire Haruka. When I hear her story, I feel like I can do anything!

C As a group, you are going to choose the Hero of the Year Award winner. Jason, Amanda, and Haruka are the choices. Read the information and discuss the questions. Give reasons for your answers.

The Hero of the Year Award . . .
- is for an everyday person.
- is given once a year.

There is only one winner. The winner meets the mayor and receives a medal.

1. Were you surprised by any of the stories?
2. Did the person help themself or others?
3. Was the person brave, generous, or kind?
4. Was their act of kindness difficult to do?

D In your group, share your choice with the class.

E WRITING Turn to the Writing appendix and read a letter nominating someone for the Hero of the Year Award. Answer the questions with a partner.

1. Who is the person?
2. What adjectives describe the person?
3. Why does the writer admire the person? What did the person do?

F You want to nominate a person for the Hero of the Year Award. Answer the questions in **E**. Then write a paragraph.

5B GOALS Now I can . . .

Narrate a story _____

Describe actions and people I admire _____

1. Yes, I can.
2. Mostly, yes.
3. Not yet.

GLOBAL VOICES

A Look at the photo and read the caption. Use the internet to find three facts about Jane Goodall. Write notes; then tell a partner.

Fact 1: _____

Fact 2: _____

Fact 3: _____

B Watch the speakers at the start of the video. Which sentence is not true?

1. Laurel, Andrés, and Laly admire Jane Goodall.

2. Jane Goodall influenced the work of Laurel, Andrés, and Laly.

3. Laurel, Andrés, and Laly worked with Jane Goodall.

C Watch the full video. Match the years with the events. One year has more than one event.

1. 1934	a. Jane watched a chimpanzee take leaves from a twig.
2. 1957	b. Jane arrived at Gombe National Park in Tanzania, Africa.
3. 1960	c. Jane received an award from Queen Elizabeth II.
4. 1977	d. Jane became UN Messenger of Peace.
5. 2002	e. Jane changed the way scientists thought about chimpanzees.
6. 2004	f. Jane was born in London, England.
	g. Jane started the Jane Goodall Institute.
	h. Jane started to work as a secretary for Louis Leakey.

D Think about your own hero. You can choose a famous person or a family member or friend. Write down four important years from their life in your notebook. Then write simple past sentences to describe what happened.

E Present your person to the class. Students should ask follow-up questions to find out more information.

Jane Goodall is a hero to many people.

6

THE MIND

LOOK AT THE PHOTO. ANSWER THE QUESTIONS.

1. Why is the woman putting her photo on the wall?
2. What do you take photos of? Why?

WARM-UP VIDEO

A Look up the verbs in a dictionary. Then read about the video. Choose the correct answer.

forget	recognize	remember

The video is about Jennifer Jarett. She never forgets a face. This means she **always remembers** / **never recognizes** people's faces.

B Read the sentences. Then watch the video. Choose the correct answers. One sentence has two answers.

1. Jennifer says she can recognize _____.
   a. people she knew as a child
   b. a store clerk from 10 years ago
   c. teachers from first grade

2. Jennifer met some people in college. Later, she met them again at a party. She remembered the people but, _____.
   a. she didn't talk to them
   b. they didn't remember her
   c. not their names

3. At her college reunion, Jennifer _____.
   a. was famous
   b. made some new friends
   c. helped her friends remember people

C What can Jennifer do? Can you do it? Tell a partner.

A visitor to Chengdu, China (home of the giant panda) puts a photo of herself on the Panda Post Office wall in memory of her trip.

GOALS

Lesson A
/ Talk about important memories
/ Express degrees of certainty

Lesson B
/ Describe sleep habits
/ Ask and answer questions about a past experience

VOCABULARY

A Read the shopping list. Then complete the task with a partner.

apples	a carton of eggs
chicken	coffee
rice	a loaf of bread
milk	butter
a bunch of bananas	orange juice

1. The words in the box were in Unit 3. Which ones do you **recognize**?

2. It is **easy to forget** a long list of words. Imagine you can't write them down or use your phone. How can you **remember** them?

WORD BANK
remember to keep information in your mind
    easy to / hard to ~
forget to not remember
    easy to / hard to ~
recognize to see and remember something from the past
memory the ability to remember things
    have a good / have a bad ~

B Look at the list in **A** for one minute. Then close your book and write as many items in your notebook as you can.

C How did you do in **B**? Complete the sentences.

1. I remembered **all** / **some** / **none** of the words.

2. I didn't remember these words: _____.

3. For me, it was **easy to** / **hard to remember** the words.

4. I think I **have a good** / **have a bad** memory.

D Compare your answers in **C** with a partner. Then take turns asking and answering the questions.

1. How did you remember the words from the list in **A**?

2. Are there words you always forget in English? Which words are easy to remember?

" To remember the words, I put similar ones together, like apples and bananas.

Students practice remembering cards for a memory competition. One useful way to do this is to think about them in smaller groups.

LISTENING

A People use word webs and flashcard apps on their smartphones to study and remember new vocabulary. Do you think they are helpful? Why?

B **Listen for details.** Listen to Omar's study tip. Complete 1–4. 🎧42

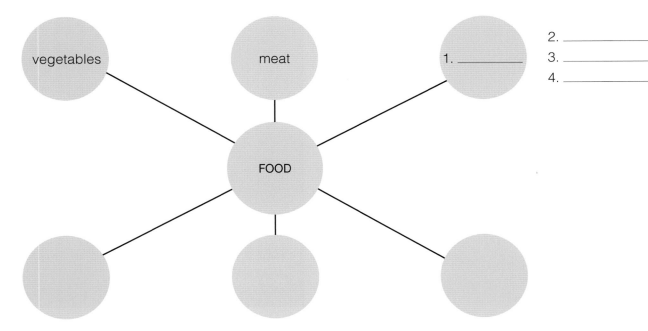

2. _____
3. _____
4. _____

C Listen to Lin's study tip. Complete the flashcard. 🎧43

Side 1

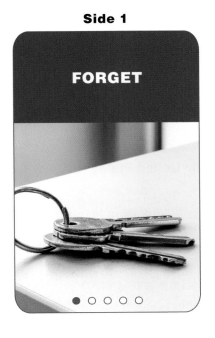

FORGET

Side 2

FORGET

Simple Past:

_____

Full Sentence:

_____
_____
_____

i **Simple Past**

Regular Verbs
learn → learned

Irregular Verbs
write → wrote

D Work with a partner. Complete the task.

1. Add more food vocabulary to the word web in **A**. Think about Omar's study tip and explain why you chose those words.

2. Use Lin's instructions to make a flashcard for the verb *write*.

E What do you do to remember vocabulary? How does this help you?

SPEAKING

A Read the conversation and listen. Then answer the questions. 🎧44

Mia: I'm so excited! Are you ready to go to the concert?

Justin: Um . . . just a minute. I can't find my phone, and the tickets are on it.

Mia: You're kidding!

Justin: No, I'm not.

Mia: Well, is your phone in your backpack?

Justin: I don't think so.

Mia: Maybe you forgot it at school today.

Justin: Maybe, I'm not sure.

Mia: Oh, Justin. Try to remember!

Justin: Wait . . . I found it. It was on the sofa, under some pillows. Come on, let's go!

1. What is Justin looking for?
2. Does he find it?

Where do you look for things you can't find?

B Practice the conversation in **A** with a partner.

C Work with a new partner. Read your questions. Write one more question for each category.

Student A	**Student B**
The Teacher	**Our School**
1. Is the teacher married?	7. Is there a bus stop near school?
2. Does the teacher like coffee?	8. Does our school have ten classrooms?
3. _____	9. _____
Our Classmate: _____	**Schools in the United States**
4. Is _____ a college student?	10. Do students wear uniforms?
5. Does _____ live near school?	11. Do students have a lot of homework?
6. _____	12. _____

D Ask your questions from **C**. Use the expressions in the Speaking Strategy to answer your partner.

❝ Is the teacher married?

Maybe, I'm not sure. ❞

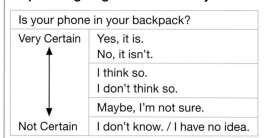

GRAMMAR

A Read the Unit 6, Lesson A Grammar Reference in the appendix. Complete the exercises. Then do the exercises below.

THE SIMPLE PAST: AFFIRMATIVE AND NEGATIVE STATEMENTS (IRREGULAR VERBS)			
Subject	*Did + Not*	Verb	
I / You / He / She / We / They		**found**	the phone.
	didn't	**find**	

B **PRONUNCIATION: Irregular Simple Past** Listen and say the verb pairs in Row A. Then guess the pronunciation of the verbs in Row B. 🎧46

Row A	forget / forgot	tell / told	ring / rang	keep / kept	understand / understood
Row B	get / got	sell / sold	sing / sang	sleep / slept	stand / stood

C Listen and check your pronunciation of the verbs in Row B. 🎧47

D Work with a partner. Use the gameboard to play Tic-tac-toe.

Student A: You are **X**. **Student B:** You are **O**.

1. **Student A:** Choose a square. Write and say the simple past form of the verb. If you are correct, put an *X* on the square. If not, leave it blank.
2. **Student B:** Do Step 1. If you are correct, put an *O* on the square.
3. Continue playing. The first person with three *X*s or *O*s in a row wins the game.
4. Use the gameboard in your partner's book. Repeat steps 1–3 to play again.

come	go	make
eat	have	speak
get	know	think

E Work with your partner. In five minutes, write as many sentences as you can with the simple past verb forms on the completed gameboard.

F With your partner, compare your sentences with another pair of students. Who wrote more? Are they correct?

G Create your own gameboard in your notebook. Choose nine other irregular verbs from the Grammar Reference in the appendix. Repeat **D–F**.

People gather in Times Square, New York City to watch a vehicle land on the planet Mars.

ACTIVE ENGLISH Try it out!

A Write the simple past form of each verb in parentheses. Check your answers with a partner.

1. I remember the first time I _____ (eat) . . .
2. I remember when I _____ (buy) . . .
3. I remember the time I _____ (go) to . . .
4. I remember the first time I _____ (see) . . .
5. I remember the day I _____ (meet) . . .
6. I remember when I _____ (get) my first job at . . .

B What are some of your memories? Complete the sentences in **A** in your notebook. Make notes so that you can talk about each memory.

> " I remember the first time I ate katsu curry. I think I was seven, but I'm not sure. Anyway, my grandmother . . .

WORD BANK
memory something you remember
  a happy / sad ~

C Work in a group of three and complete the task. One person should be the timekeeper.

1. Choose a sentence from **A** for the group to talk about.
2. Each student has one minute to tell the group their story.
3. After everyone speaks, answer the questions.
   a. What is something you learned about the people in your group?
   b. Were your three stories similar? If yes, how?

> " Ruben bought a motorcycle last year. I didn't know that.

> Our stories were similar. We all had happy memories! "

D In the same group of three students, repeat the task in **C** with four other sentences from **A**.

E Share one story from your group with the class.

6A GOALS   Now I can . . .

Talk about important memories _____	1. Yes, I can.
Express degrees of certainty _____	2. Mostly, yes.
	3. Not yet.

VOCABULARY

A Say the verbs in the Word Bank with your teacher. Which ones do you know? Look up new words in a dictionary. Then discuss the meanings with your class.

WORD BANK
sleep ←→ wake up
fall asleep ←→ stay awake

B Read the sentences with a partner. Then choose **T** for *true* or **F** for *false*. Explain your answers.

1. Adults need to **sleep** more than teenagers.   T   F
2. It's good to **go to bed** and **wake up** at the same time each day.   T   F
3. When you can't **fall asleep**, it helps to read something on your phone.   T   F
4. When you exercise before bed, you sleep well.   T   F
5. Most people do not **dream** when they sleep.   T   F
6. When you're sleeping, your body **rests**, but your brain is very busy.   T   F

" I think number one is true.

Really? I think teenagers need to sleep more. **"**

C Check your answers for **B** in the Information Gap Activities appendix. How many were correct?

D With your partner, use the words in blue to write a discussion question about sleep. Post your question for the class.

E Choose three of your classmates' questions from **D**. Answer them with your partner.

During a long car ride, is it hard for you to stay awake?

A STUDY OF SLEEP

It's 3:30 in the morning. You went to bed at 10:00 p.m., but then you woke up at 3:00. Now it's 3:30, and you're still awake. It's so strange. You're not hungry or thirsty or worried about anything. You try to rest, but you can't fall asleep. Why? There may be a surprising answer.

Dr. Thomas Wehr did an experiment to research sleep. During the winter, he put people in a room with no light from lamps, TVs, or computers. Then, during the night, he studied the people's sleep patterns.[1]

What happened? The people went to bed, but they didn't fall asleep right away. Most stayed awake for two hours. Next, the people slept for four to five hours. Then they woke up, and they stayed awake and were active[2] for one to three hours. Finally, the people slept again for four to five hours.

Dr. Wehr discovered a new sleep pattern. But maybe it's not new. In the past, before electric light, many people slept this way, say scientists. Nowadays, we sleep in a different way.

So, the next time you wake up in the middle of the night and can't sleep, relax! Your sleep patterns may be normal after all. 🎧48

[1] A **pattern** is a repeated or regular way something happens.
[2] When you are **active**, you move around and don't feel tired.

A The article is about a sleep study. Read the first paragraph. What was the aim of the study? Guess.

B **Identify the main idea.** Read the article. Then choose the main point.

1. Today, people have healthier sleep patterns.
2. Waking up at night is not good for you.
3. It's normal to wake up at night.
4. Sleep research has a lot of problems.

C Read the article quickly to find answers to complete the chart.

Activity	Time
People were in bed but were awake.	2 hours
People slept.	
	1–3 hours
	4–5 hours

D Answer the questions with a partner.

1. In your opinion, is the sleep pattern in the article healthy? Why or why not?
2. Do you ever wake up at night? When it happens, what do you do?

Wehr's study shows how electric light changes sleep patterns, but electric light can also make us tired during the day. Here, a person takes a nap inside a sleeping pod at work.

LISTENING

A Answer the questions. Then tell a partner.

1. What time do you usually wake up?
2. What time do you usually go to bed?
3. Are you most energetic in the morning, in the afternoon, or at night?

B Read the information. Which animal are you? Tell your partner.

Michael Breus is a sleep doctor. He wrote a book about four different sleep and energy patterns. He gave each one an animal's name.			
Are you a **bear**?	Are you a **lion**?	Are you a **wolf**?	Are you a **dolphin**?

These people are most energetic in the late morning.	These people go to bed around 9:00 p.m.	These people are most energetic at night.	These people wake up early.

C Write the information from **B** in the chart. Then listen and complete the chart. 🎧49

	Wake Up	Most Energetic	Go to Bed
Bears	_____ a.m.	_____late_____ morning	_____ p.m.
Lions	_____ a.m.	_____ morning	_____ p.m.
Wolves	_____late_____	at _____	_____ (or later)
Dolphins	_____ morning	_____ times	_____ at night

D Listen again. Match the animals and the characteristics. One animal has two characteristics. 🎧49

1. Bears   a. emotional
2. Lions   b. smart
3. Wolves   c. friendly
4. Dolphins   d. nervous
                  e. hardworking

E Which animal are you? Did your answer in **B** change or stay the same? Why?

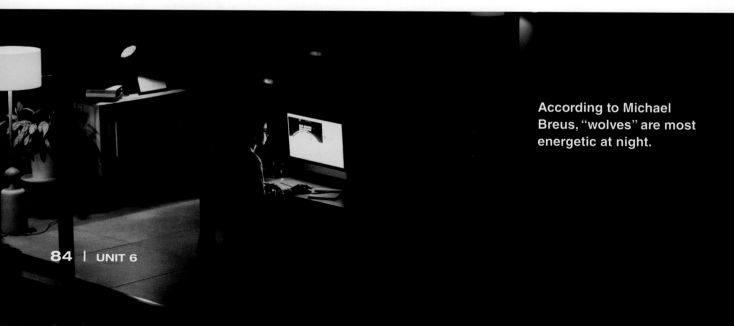

According to Michael Breus, "wolves" are most energetic at night.

GRAMMAR

A Read the Unit 6, Lesson B Grammar Reference in the appendix. Complete the exercises. Then do the exercises below.

Did	Subject	Verb		Short Answers
THE SIMPLE PAST: *YES / NO* **QUESTIONS**				
Did	you he they	**rest** **wake up**	last night?	Yes, I did. / *No, I didn't.* Yes, he did. / *No, he didn't.* Yes, they did. / *No, they didn't.*

Wh- word	Did	Subject	Verb	Answers
THE SIMPLE PAST: *WH-* **QUESTIONS**				
When	**did**	you she they	**study**?	(I / She / They studied) last night.
			wake up?	(I / She / They woke up) at seven.
What			**happened**?	I woke up late this morning.

B Complete the conversation with simple past questions and answers using the words in parentheses. Then practice the conversation with a partner.

A: (1.) _____Did you go out_____ (you / go out) last night?

B: No, (2.) _____. I (3.) _____ (stay) home and (4.) _____ (watch) a movie.

A: Really? (5.) _____ (what / you / watch)?

B: An old zombie movie.

A: (6.) _____ (you / like) it?

B: Yes, (7.) _____, but later I (8.) _____ (have) a bad dream.

A: (9.) _____ (why / you / have) a bad dream?

B: Because it was a very scary movie! (10.) _____ (what / you / do) last night?

A: I (11.) _____ (go) to a party.

B: (12.) _____ (who / you / go) with?

A: Margo.

B: (13.) _____ (you / have) fun?

A: Yeah, we (14.) _____ (have) a great time at first. But then, something strange happened.

C What strange thing happened to Speaker A in **B**? Continue the conversation with a partner. Ask and answer four more simple past questions.

D With your partner, role-play your conversation for another pair of students. Whose story is the best?

Visitors stay up all night to visit an art event in Toronto, Canada.

ACTIVE ENGLISH Try it out!

A Think about your sleep patterns for the last three days. Complete the chart.

	Yesterday	Two Days Ago	Three Days Ago
Time I woke up			
Time I went to bed			

B Use the words to write simple past *Yes / No* or *Wh-* questions in your notebook. Then ask a partner the questions and take notes.

1. what time / you / get up?
2. when / you / go to bed?
3. you / fall asleep / right away?
4. you / exercise or look at your phone / before bed?
5. how many / hours / you / sleep?
6. what / you / dream / about?

C Reread the six sleep facts in the Information Gap Activities appendix. Then answer the questions with your partner.

1. Do you and your partner have good sleep habits? Why or why not? Use your notes from **B** to explain.
2. What are two things you can do to sleep better?

D Share your answers from **C** with the class.

E **WRITING** Read the paragraph in the Writing appendix. Then answer the questions.

1. When did the writer stay up late?
2. Why did the writer stay up late?
3. What happened that night? Use the words to explain.

   at six in the evening   at midnight   at 3:00 a.m.   three hours later
4. How did the writer feel at the end? Why?

WORD BANK
stay up to stay awake

F Answer the questions in **E** about yourself. Then use your answers to write a paragraph.

6B GOALS   Now I can . . .

Describe sleep habits _____	1. Yes, I can.
Ask and answer questions about a past experience _____	2. Mostly, yes.
	3. Not yet.

GLOBAL VOICES

A Watch the video. Then choose **T** for *true* and **F** for *false*.

1. Neil deGrasse Tyson sleeps for five and a half hours a day.   **T**   **F**

2. On the weekends, he sleeps for seven hours.   **T**   **F**

3. He likes to take naps.   **T**   **F**

4. He thinks sleep is a good use of time.   **T**   **F**

> **WORD BANK**
>
> **sleep in** to wake up later than usual
>
> **take a nap** to sleep for a short time during the day
>
> **a waste of time** not a good use of time

B Read. Then watch the video again and complete the sentences.

Neil: Imagine explaining sleep to an alien.

Alien: What are you going to do now?

Neil: Well, I'm going to lay down and be semi-comatose for a (1.) _____ of a day. Check back with me later.

Alien: What?! Why?

Neil: (2.) _____. My body (3.) _____.

Alien: Why?

Neil: (4.) _____!

C In Neil deGrasse Tyson's opinion, is sleep easy to explain? Why or why not?

D Answer the questions in your notebook.

1. How many hours do you sleep per day?

2. Do you sleep in on the weekends? Why or why not?

3. Do you ever take a nap? When?

E Explain your answers in **D** to a partner. Are you similar or different?

Neil deGrasse Tyson is a scientist who studies space.

REAL WORLD LINK PROFILE A ROLE MODEL

Greta Thunberg speaks to the media in Madrid, Spain. Many people think Greta is a role model.

A Read the information. Then look at the person in the photo. What do you know about her?

> **Role models** are people we admire. They . . .
> - do good things and help people.
> - are good teachers. We can learn from them.
> - can be world leaders, scientists, artists, and many other things.

B Now read about the person in the photo. Complete the sentences with the simple past forms of the verbs in parentheses.

Greta Thunberg is a young Swedish climate champion. In high school, Greta (1.) _____was_____ (be) very worried about climate change.* She (2.) _____ (decide) to do something about it. She (3.) _____ (leave) school, and she (4.) _____ (talk) to politicians and business leaders. In 2019, she (5.) _____ (take) a trip: She (6.) _____ (travel) from the UK to the US on a boat. In the US, she (7.) _____ (speak) at the United Nations, and she (8.) _____ (go) to a big meeting on climate change.

*Climate change *is the warming of the Earth.*

C Work with a partner. Unscramble the words to make questions. Then ask and answer the questions. Do you think Greta is a good role model?

1. worried about / in high school / was / what / Greta

   <u>What was Greta worried about in high school?</u>

2. did / leave / why / school / she

   _____

3. about / who / talk to / did / climate change / she

   _____

4. she / take / in 2019 / did / a trip

   _____

5. go / where / did / she

   _____

6. did / speak / she / where

   _____

7. she / by airplane / did / in 2019 / travel

   _____

8. what / she / did / meeting / kind of / go to

   _____

D You are going to introduce a role model. Complete the task.

1. Choose a role model. This should be a famous person (who other people know—not a parent, friend, or teacher).

2. Answer the questions.

   - What is the person's name?
   - Where and when was the person born?
   - What is the person's job now?
   - Why did you choose this person as a role model? What did he or she do?

E **You Choose** Choose an option to tell others about your role model. Use your notes from **D**.

Option 1 Write a paragraph about the person.

Option 2 Make a short video or audio presentation. Record yourself talking about your role model.

Option 3 Create a photo or video collage about your role model. Use sentences to explain each image.

F Work in a small group. Complete the task.

One student: Present your profile.

Other students: Listen. Then answer the question.

Is the person a good role model? Why or why not?

Different forms of transportation move around downtown Taipei.

GOALS

Lesson A
/ Talk about places in a neighborhood
/ Explain location

Lesson B
/ Talk about city traffic
/ Explain how to get around a city

CITY LIFE

LOOK AT THE PHOTO. ANSWER THE QUESTIONS.

1. What types of transportation can you see?
2. How do you move around your town or city?

WARM-UP VIDEO

A The video is about the old downtown area of Tokyo, Japan. The title is *Nothing is Lost*. What do you think it is about?

B Watch the video. Choose the things you see.

markets	taxis	trains
subways	temples	trees

C Watch the video again. Choose the correct answers.

1. In the Kanda neighborhood, life moves **slowly / quickly**.
2. The streets **are / aren't** wide.
3. There are many **small / large** restaurants.
4. In the part of the neighborhood near the university, people can buy **electronics / books**.
5. It's **easy / not easy** to make old things.
6. In Kanda, people **want to / don't want to** change how they live.

D Choose the correct answer.

If something warms the heart, *it . . .*

1. changes how you feel.
2. gives you a happy feeling.
3. makes you do old things.

E Do you think it's important to keep old neighborhoods the same? Why or why not?

People take the subway in Stockholm, Sweden.

VOCABULARY

A Look at the **subway station** in the photo. What train stations do you know? When are they busy?

B Work on your own. Complete the task.

1. Look at the places in the Word Bank. Look up any new words in a dictionary.
2. Match the words below.
3. Add the words to the Word Bank.

   1. **bus**
   2. **department**
   3. **gas**   a. **club**
   4. **grocery**   b. **salon**
   5. **hair**   c. **station**
   6. **night**   d. **store**
   7. **police**
   8. **subway**

WORD BANK

bookstore

_____
_____

train station

_____
_____
_____
_____

health club (gym)

_____

nail salon

_____

C Work with a partner. Discuss the questions.

1. Which places in **B** do you go to?
2. When do you go to these places? What do you do there?

> 66 | I go to the train station early in the morning. I take the train to school.

LISTENING

A **PRONUNCIATION: Stress in Compound Nouns** Listen and repeat. Underline the stress in the nouns? 🎧50

1. bookstore
2. bus station
3. grocery store
4. nightclub
5. gas station
6. hair salon

> **ℹ Compound Nouns**
> *bookstore* (one word)
> *grocery store* (two words)

B Yuki meets Pablo on the street. Listen to the first part of their conversation. Then complete the task. 🎧51

| Yuki | bookstore | gym | hair salon | library | restaurant | subway station |
| Pablo | bookstore | gym | hair salon | library | restaurant | subway station |

1. Where did each person go? Underline the place.
2. Where are they going next? Circle the place.
3. Where do you think Pablo goes next? Guess.

C Listen to the full conversation. Write **Y** for *Yuki*, **P** for *Pablo*, or **B** for *both Yuki and Pablo*. 🎧52

1. _____ live(s) in the neighborhood.
2. _____ think(s) the neighborhood is convenient.
3. _____ has / have a lot of homework.
4. _____ want(s) to buy a magazine.
5. _____ doesn't / don't like coffee.

D Read the sentences. Guess the missing words. Then listen to the full conversation again and check your answers. 🎧52

1. a. How are _____?
   b. How's it _____?
2. a. Is _____ your neighborhood?
   b. Do you _____ around here?
3. a. Where are you _____ right now?
   b. Where are you _____ to?
4. a. You can _____ a cup of coffee.
   b. I don't really _____ coffee.
5. a. Don't _____ to me.
   b. _____ talking allowed.

E Work with a partner. Make a conversation about your neighborhood. Use some of the questions in **D**. Then perform your conversation for the class.

The Ateneo Grand Splendid bookstore in Buenos Aires, Argentina was a theater in the past.

SPEAKING

A Read the conversation and listen. Adam and Jan are driving. What are they looking for? Where is it? 🎧53

Adam: What's that noise? Something sounds funny.

Jan: Uh-oh. I think we're running out of gas.

Adam: That's not good.

Jan: We have to find a gas station. Do you know this neighborhood?

Adam: Yeah, I know it pretty well.

Jan: Great! Where's the nearest gas station?

Adam: There's one on Court Street, I think.

Jan: OK. How do I get there from here?

Adam: Go straight and turn right on First Avenue. Go one block. It's on the right, on the corner of Court Street and First Avenue.

A **block** is the space between streets. The **corner** is where two streets meet.

B Practice the conversation in **A** with a partner.

C Work with your partner. Start at the **X**. Go from 1 to 7 in order. Take turns giving directions.

1. gas station
2. Bridge Theater
3. Carl's Cafe
4. library
5. Pat's Hair Salon
6. Jimmy's Gym
7. bookstore

SPEAKING STRATEGY 🎧54
Asking for and Giving Directions

Are you familiar with this neighborhood? / Do you know this neighborhood?

Is there a gas station near here?
    Yes, there's one on First Avenue. /
    Yes, it's on first Avenue.

Where's the nearest gas station?
    There's one on First Avenue. /
    It's on First Avenue.

How do I get there from here?
    Go straight. / Turn right. / Turn left.
    It's on the right / left.
    It's on the corner.

❝ I'm at the gas station. How do I get to the Bridge Theater from here?

Turn right on Court Street. Go one block. Then turn left . . . **❞**

GRAMMAR

A Read the Unit 7, Lesson A Grammar Reference in the appendix. Complete the exercises. Then do the exercises below.

PREPOSITIONS OF PLACE: *AT, ON,* AND *IN*	
A: Where are you? **B:** I'm **at** school. I'm **on** the second floor, **in** my classroom.	• Use **at** + building: **at the mall, at home** • Use **on** + floor: **on the top floor** • Use **in** + room: **in my office, in the kitchen**
A: Where is the gas station? **B:** It's **at** 30 First Avenue. / It's **on** First Avenue.	• Use **at** + address: **at 100 Smith Street** • Use **on** + street: **on Smith Street**

B Work with a partner. Complete the task.

1. Read the email to Amy from the university. Underline the places.

2. Find the places on the map on the previous page.

3. Use the words in the box to complete the email.

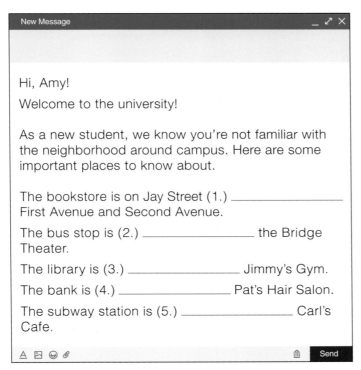

New Message

Hi, Amy!

Welcome to the university!

As a new student, we know you're not familiar with the neighborhood around campus. Here are some important places to know about.

The bookstore is on Jay Street (1.) _____ First Avenue and Second Avenue.

The bus stop is (2.) _____ the Bridge Theater.

The library is (3.) _____ Jimmy's Gym.

The bank is (4.) _____ Pat's Hair Salon.

The subway station is (5.) _____ Carl's Cafe.

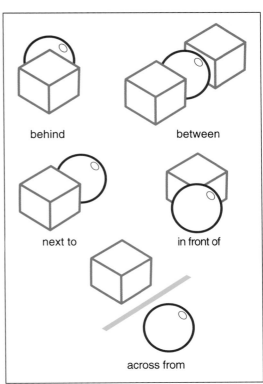

behind   between

next to   in front of

across from

C Amy has two messages. Find the **hair salon** and the **library** on the map. Then complete the messages with *at, on, in,* and the words from the box in **B**.

Message One

Hi, Amy. This is Pat's Hair Salon. You have an appointment tomorrow at 2:00 p.m. We're (1.) _____ 200 Jay Street—that's (2.) _____ Jay Street, (3.) _____ Second Avenue and Third Avenue. We're (4.) _____ the middle of the block, (5.) _____ the bank. See you tomorrow!

Message Two

Hi, Amy. Our study group is meeting tonight (6.) _____ the library. We're meeting (7.) _____ the back room (8.) _____ the second floor. Remember, the library is (9.) _____ the gym (10.) _____ First Avenue. It's not (11.) _____ the corner—it's (12.) _____ the middle of the block. Hope to see you later!

305   304

The neighbors at 50 Dean Street: Ms. Smith,
Ms. Sanchez, Mr. Hu, Ms. Jones, Dr. Lewis, and Mr. Busby.

A   Read the information. What do the police find? Why is it important?

> Ms. Smith and Ms. Jones live on the third floor in the same apartment building at 50 Dean Street. They have tea together every Thursday afternoon at four o'clock.
>
> One Thursday, Ms. Smith doesn't answer the doorbell. Ms. Jones calls the building manager, Mr. Busby. He has a key to Ms. Smith's apartment. He opens the door and sees Ms. Smith on the floor. She is dead! Who is the killer?
>
> The police ask the neighbors, "Where were you on Thursday afternoon?" Each neighbor has a story: Mr. Hu was at the gym; Ms. Sanchez was at the office; Dr. Lewis was at the hospital; and so on. Someone is lying!
>
> Later, the police find an apartment key under Ms. Smith's sofa. The number on the key is 300. The key belongs to the killer.

B   Work with your partner to find the killer. Try to be the first in the class.

Student A: Read the sentences to your partner.

Student B: Write the names and room numbers on the doors.

Ms. Smith lives in apartment 305.

Mr. Busby lives across from Ms. Smith.

Ms. Sanchez lives between Dr. Lewis and Mr. Busby.

Mr. Hu lives across from Ms. Sanchez.

The apartment next to Ms. Smith's is 303.

Mr. Hu lives next to Ms. Jones.

Ms. Jones lives across from apartment 300.

7A **GOALS**   Now I can . . .

Talk about places in a neighborhood _____	1. Yes, I can.
Explain location _____	2. Mostly, yes.
	3. Not yet.

7B ▸ IN THE CITY

VOCABULARY

A Read the information. Pay attention to the words in blue.

> During rush hour* in many cities, there are a lot of cars on the road. There are **delays**, and people are often stuck in **traffic**. Their cars don't move. In **heavy traffic**, a 30-minute **journey** can sometimes take an hour. There is nothing fun about being stuck in traffic. It's annoying, and it **pollutes** the air.
>
> Cities have many different kinds of **transportation systems**. Which one do you think is best for moving **passengers** across a city quickly and cheaply?

__Rush hour__ is the busy time at the beginning and end of the day when people travel to and from work.

WORD BANK
heavy ⟷ light
pollute (verb)
polluted (adjective)
pollution (noun)
traffic

B Ask and answer the questions about the information in **A** with a partner.

1. Describe *stuck in traffic* in your own words. When does it usually happen?
2. What does the text say about *heavy traffic*?
3. What pollutes the air?
4. What are some examples of transportation systems?
5. Which transportation system do you think is best? Why?

❝ Rush hour starts around six-thirty in the morning. The traffic is bad, and the trains are crowded then, too.

C Choose your answers for where you live. Then discuss with your partner.

How is the traffic during rush hour?	**heavy**	**so-so**	**light**
How is the air?	**very polluted**	**so-so**	**not very polluted**
How is the transportation system?	**terrible**	**so-so**	**excellent**

A train beats the traffic in Taipei. Trains don't get stuck in heavy traffic like cars.

LET'S GO ON
THE METRO!

People in the Dominican Republic are on the road a lot. They take taxis to business meetings. They take mini vans and motorbike taxis to go shopping. They take local buses to school and long-distance buses to visit family outside of the big cities. In the capital city, they also take the subway—the Santo Domingo Metro.

The Santo Domingo Metro is not an old system. It opened in 2009 and now has two lines with a total of 34 subway stations. The subway system is 48.5 kilometers (around 30 miles) long. Every day of the week, the metro runs from 6:00 a.m. until 10:30 p.m. In 2014, passengers took the metro over 61 million times. The metro is a popular form of transportation in central areas of the city.

The Santo Domingo Metro in the Dominican Republic opened in 2009.

Why do you think subways are popular in cities like Santo Domingo? Well, for one thing, they're convenient. Also, subway passengers don't have to worry about traffic delays. Their journey can be quick and quiet. People can save time and money.

Subway systems are good for cities, too. In most cities, there are a lot of people living in a small area. They are often traveling short distances[1] and going to the same places. Subways can move many people easily from place to place. Also, when more people ride the subway, there aren't as many cars on the road. That helps with the problem of air pollution.

The metro is changing how people move about Santo Domingo. Like all big cities, traffic is still heavy, and there is more work to do. The city has plans to build new stations and four more metro lines. Projects like this can take a long time, but they are worth the wait! 🎧55b

[1]**Distance** is the space between two things.

A The article is about the Santo Domingo Metro system in the Dominican Republic. Before you read, guess what the numbers mean. Do not write your answers yet.

1. 2009 _____
2. 6:00–10:30 _____
3. 48.5 _____
4. 2 _____
5. 34 _____

B **Summarize.** Read the first two paragraphs. Summarize the second paragraph by writing a sentence for each item in **A**.

C Read the rest of the article. Why are metro systems popular? Why are they good for cities? Complete the sentences.

1. Metro systems are _convenient_ .
2. On the subway, passengers don't worry about _____.
3. They can have a _____ and _____ journey.
4. People can save _____ and _____.
5. _____ people can easily move from place to place.
6. There are not as _____ cars on the road. That helps with air _____.

D Work with a partner. Complete the task.

1. Reread the first paragraph of the article. What are the different forms of transportation in Santo Domingo?

   _____   _____
   _____   _____
   _____

2. Which forms of transportation do you have in your city? Which ones do you use? Why?

Many people visit Vermont to see the trees change color in the fall.

LISTENING

A Answer the questions with a partner.

1. In what country is the state of Vermont? Guess.

2. Look at the photo. What do you see?

B **Listen for context.** Listen. Choose the correct answer to complete the sentence. 🎧56

You are listening to _____ .

a. a news report   c. an interview

b. an advertisement   d. a class lecture

C Read the sentences. Then listen again and choose the correct words. 🎧56

1. The state of Vermont is **very polluted** / **not polluted**.

2. The capital city has a **small** / **large** population.

3. During rush hour in Vermont's capital city, most people **are** / **aren't** stuck in traffic.

4. Vermont is famous for its sweet **maple syrup** / **ice cream**.

5. There are a lot of things to do **outdoors** / **indoors** all over the state.

D Answer the questions with a partner.

1. Do you want to visit Vermont? Why or why not?

2. Is there an area in your country like Vermont? What is its population? What is it famous for? Do you like this place?

GRAMMAR

A Read the Unit 7, Lesson B Grammar Reference in the appendix. Complete the exercises. Then do the exercises below.

QUESTIONS AND ANSWERS WITH *HOW MANY* (PLURAL COUNT NOUNS)	
How many cars are there?	
There are **a lot / many / some / a few**. There aren't **many / any**.	A lot. / Many. / Some. / A few. Not many. / None.
QUESTIONS AND ANSWERS WITH *HOW MUCH* (NONCOUNT NOUNS)	
How much pollution is there?	
There is **a lot / some / a little**. There isn't **much / any**.	A lot. / Some. / A little. Not much. / None.
How many is used to ask about plural count nouns. *How much* is used to ask about noncount nouns.	

B Complete the questions with *much* or *many* and the correct form of the verb *be*. Then think about answers to the questions for where you live.

1. How _____ people _____ there?

2. How _____ pollution _____ there in the air today?

3. How _____ large parks _____ there?

4. How _____ taxis _____ there?

5. How _____ noise _____ there?

6. How _____ fun things to do at night _____ there?

7. How _____ tall buildings _____ there?

8. How _____ hot days _____ there?

9. How _____ rush hour traffic _____ there?

C Work with a partner. Ask and answer the questions in **B** for where you live.

" How many large parks are there in your city?

Not many. I can only think of two. "

D In your opinion, is your town / city a good place to live? Why or why not? Use your answers in **C** to explain.

" It's a good place to live, but there isn't a lot of open space. There are only two large parks.

Chapultepec Forest is a large park in Mexico City.

There can be a lot to see in a short time in a big city like Paris, France.

ACTIVE ENGLISH Try it out!

A Read about Neil. Complete the questions below with *many* or *much*. Then answer the questions with short answers.

> Neil is an old family friend. He is visiting a city you know well. His flight arrives at 9:00 a.m. on Friday. He leaves at 12:00 p.m. the next day. He has a small suitcase and a backpack. Neil wants to go sightseeing alone, but he doesn't know anything about the city, and he only speaks English.

1. How _____ time does Neil have in your city?   _____

2. How _____ days does he have?   _____

3. How _____ words in your language does he know?   _____

4. How _____ bags does he have?   _____

5. How _____ information about your city does he have?   _____

B Make a plan for Neil. Write your ideas in the chart.

1. Neil needs to get from the airport to his hotel. What is the best form of transportation?

2. Neil wants to do three fun things in your city. What should he see? How can he get around? Can you give him some tips?

Airport → Hotel	
Tip #1	
Tip #2	
Tip #3	

C Role-play with a partner. Take turns being Neil. Then switch roles and do it again.

" I arrive on Friday morning. How do I get from the airport to my hotel? Are there any taxis?

There are some taxis, but they're expensive. You can . . . "

D WRITING Write a plan for a one-day visitor to your town / city. Turn to the Writing appendix to see an example. Then write your plan.

1. How does the visitor get from the airport to your city?

2. What one thing should they see or do in your city?

7B GOALS Now I can . . .

Talk about city traffic _____

Explain how to get around a city _____

1. Yes, I can.
2. Mostly, yes.
3. Not yet.

GLOBAL VOICES

A Read the information. What types of transportation do you think you can find in Seoul?

> Seoul is a megacity. A megacity is a city that has a population of over ten million people.

B Watch the video. Choose the sentence that is true.

1. Seven million people pass though Seoul Station every day.
2. Seoul Station is a train station and a subway station.
3. People can only catch taxis at Seoul Station.

C Watch the video again. Match each bus with the correct information.

1. Blue buses . . .   a. travel around the downtown area and stop at popular parts of the city.
2. Green buses . . .   b. connect Seoul with other areas outside of the city.
3. Yellow buses . . .   c. connect residential areas, subway stations, and bus stations.
4. Red Buses . . .   d. travel across Seoul and connect different parts of the city.

D Watch the video one more time. Choose **T** for *true* and **F** for *false*.

1. Not many people take regular taxis in Seoul because they are expensive.   **T**   **F**
2. Bullet trains travel at speeds of over 150 miles per hour.   **T**   **F**
3. There are 20 subway lines that cover 1,000 miles of track.   **T**   **F**
4. You can buy electronics in some subway stations.   **T**   **F**

E Use your phone to find facts about another megacity. Then write four *true* / *false* sentences. Say your sentences to a partner, who will guess if the statements are true or false. Then switch roles.

**People board a bus
in Seoul, South Korea.**

ALL ABOUT YOU

LOOK AT THE PHOTO. ANSWER THE QUESTIONS.

1. What do you think the person does in their spare time?

2. What word can you use to describe the person's personality?

WARM-UP VIDEO

A Look at the activities. Which ones do you know? Look up new words in a dictionary.

biking	running
climbing	playing video games
making movies	writing / telling stories

B Watch the video with the sound off. Choose the activities Fitz Cahall is doing in **A**.

C Watch the video with the sound on. Choose the correct answers.

1. Fitz loves to be **in the city** / **outside**.

2. He spent **a month** / **a couple of months** on the road.

3. He had many stories, but he couldn't **write** / **sell** them.

4. He **created a job** / **got a job at a school**.

5. He started a radio show; later, he made **films** / **money**.

D Answer the questions with a partner.

1. How does Fitz use his interests in his job?

2. Are you similar to Fitz in any way? Why or why not?

A toy collector is surrounded by his collection.

GOALS

Lesson A
/ Talk about different sports
/ Invite others to do something

Lesson B
/ Describe your personality
/ Talk about how often you do something

VOCABULARY

A Say the sports in the Word Bank. Then write the name of each sport under the correct picture. What other sports do you know?

WORD BANK

baseball	running
basketball	skateboarding
biking	soccer
field hockey	surfing
golf	swimming
(rock) climbing	tennis

B Work with a partner. Complete the task.

1. **Student A:** Choose six sports from the Word Bank. Perform them.
   Student B: Say the sports your partner performs.

2. Change roles. Repeat Step 1.

3. Repeat steps 1 and 2. This time, close your books.

C Read the information note. Then write the sports from the Word Bank in the chart.

Go	Play
biking	baseball

i Using Go and Play

Use *go* and *play* to talk about doing a sport.

go + *-ing* word: **go biking**

play + a game: **play baseball**

D Work with a partner. Take turns asking and answering the questions.

1. Do you play any sports? Which one(s)?

2. Do you ever go _____? When was the last time?

66 Do you play any sports?

Yes. Sometimes, I play basketball with my friends on the weekend. / No, not really. But I watch soccer a lot. 99

LISTENING

A Look at the title of the text in **B** and the photo at the bottom of the page. What do you think the story is about?

B Listen to the first part of the story and complete the text. Then answer the question. 🎧57

> **From Physician¹ to Beach Bum²**
>
> In the 1950s, Dorian "Doc" Paskowitz was a successful physician. He was handsome and in good health. To many people, Doc's life seemed perfect. But it wasn't. Doc was
> (1.) _____. He didn't like his work. The one thing he loved was (2.) _____.
> So one day, Doc decided to change his life. He decided to follow his (3.) _____.

¹A **physician** is a doctor.
²A **beach bum** is a person who spends a lot of time at the beach.

What do you think happened to Doc Paskowitz and his family? Choose your answer(s). Then explain your ideas to a partner.

a. He went surfing all the time.   c. He traveled with his family.

b. He became a doctor in another city.   d. He built a house on the beach.

C **Listen for details.** Listen to the second part of the story. Choose the correct answers. 🎧58

1. They lived . . .

   a. in a small camper.   b. a busy life.

2. They visited places like . . .

   a. California and Australia.   b. Mexico and Venezuela.

3. The family had . . .

   a. a lot of money.   b. a small business.

4. The children did not . . .

   a. go to school.   b. learn to surf well.

D Listen to the second part of the story again. Complete each sentence with one word. 🎧58

1. Doc and his wife had _____ children.

2. The family became a _____ surfing family.

E What do you think of Doc and his family? Did they have a good life? Why or why not? Tell a partner.

Baja California, Mexico is a popular surfing destination.

Members of the UAE Cycling Girls Club ride their bikes together in Dubai, United Arab Emirates.

SPEAKING

A Read the conversation and listen. Then complete the task. 🎧59

Ines: Hey, Gina. I'm going biking with some friends.

Gina: That sounds fun! Where are you going?

Ines: Riverside Park. Do you want to come?

Gina: Thanks, but I can't. I need to study.

Ines: For how long?

Gina: Another hour or so.

Ines: Well, do you want to meet us later?

Gina: Sure, sounds good.

Ines: OK, text me when you're done.

Gina: I will. See you soon!

1. What does Ines invite Gina to do?

2. Underline the two ways Ines invites Gina.

3. Circle Gina's replies.

B Practice the conversation in **A** with a partner.

C Practice the conversation in **A** again. This time, use other expressions to invite and respond.

SPEAKING STRATEGY 🎧60
Inviting Others to do Something

Inviting		Saying *Yes*	Saying *No*
Do you want to	come?	(Sure,) sounds good.	(Thanks, but) I can't.
Would you like to		(Sure,) I'd love to.	I'd love to, but . . .
Would you like to . . . is a little more formal than *Do you want to*.			

D Complete the task. Choose an activity from the box or another activity with *go* or *play*.

Play	Go
cards	hiking
pool	rollerblading
video games	skiing

1. Activity I like to do: _____

2. Place to do it: _____

E Make your own conversation with your partner. Complete the task. Then perform your conversation for another pair of students.

1. Invite your partner to do your activity.

2. Your partner should first say *no* to the invitation.

3. Next, your partner accepts it.

4. Switch roles and repeat.

GRAMMAR

A Read the Unit 8, Lesson A Grammar Reference in the appendix. Complete the exercises. Then do the exercises below.

VERB + INFINITIVE / VERB + NOUN			
Subject	Verb	Infinitive	
I	**need**	to study	for a test.
She	**wants**	to meet	her friends later.
They	**like**	to go	biking together.
Subject	Verb	Noun	
I	**need**	help	with my homework.
She	**wants**	a new bike.	
They	**like**	biking	together.
Verbs followed by an infinitive (*to* + verb) or a noun: *forget, hate, learn, like, love, need, decide, plan, prepare, want*			

B Complete each sentence. Write *to* or nothing in the blank. Then check your answers with a partner.

1. I want _____ join a gym.

2. I like _____ baseball, but I don't like _____ play it.

3. I learned _____ swim as a child.

4. I love _____ dance music, but my parents hate _____ it.

5. I always forget _____ do my homework.

6. I plan _____ study English next term.

7. I'm preparing _____ take the TOEFL exam.

8. My mom really needs _____ a vacation.

9. My friends and I want _____ go swimming this weekend.

C Choose the sentences in **B** that use an infinitive.

D PRONUNCIATION: Reduced *To* and *Want to* Listen to each sentence and repeat. Notice the pronunciation. 🎧61

> **ℹ Reduced *To***
>
> In speaking, *to* is often shortened in a sentence.
>
> Don't write /tə/ or wanna.

to → /tə/   I like <u>to</u> ski.

want to → wanna   Do you <u>want to</u> come with us?

E Now listen to the sentences in **B** that use infinitives and repeat. 🎧62

F Are the sentences in **B** true for you? Take turns telling a partner. Explain your answers.

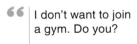

❝ I don't want to join a gym. Do you?

Yes. I need to exercise more! ❞

Friends ride skateboards together in Los Angeles, United States.

ACTIVE ENGLISH Try it out!

A Read the questions. Write your answers under *My Answer* in the chart.

	My Answer	Classmate's Name	Classmate's Answer
What's your favorite sport or event to watch?			
Which sport or activity do you like to do?			
What do you want for your birthday?			
What do you want to do this summer?			
What is one thing you learned in the last year?			
Where do you plan to go next year?			

B For each question, interview a different classmate. Write each person's name and their answer in the chart.

C Work in groups of three. For each question, read a classmate's answer. Do not say the person's name. The other students in your group should guess who gave the answer.

> **"** I asked, "What sport or activity do you like to do?" This person loves skateboarding.
>
> I know! That's Amelia. **"**
>
> **"** Yes, that's right!

D Think about the answers you heard. Answer the questions.

1. Which answers were the most common?
2. Which answer was the most interesting? Why?

8A GOALS Now I can . . .

Talk about different sports _____

Invite others to do something _____

1. Yes, I can.
2. Mostly, yes.
3. Not yet.

VOCABULARY

A Look at the words in blue. Say them with your teacher.

Penny is very **neat**. Her apartment is always clean.	Pearl is kind of **messy**. Her apartment usually isn't clean.
Penny is really **ambitious**. In the future, she wants to have her own company.	Pearl is very **easy-going** about life and work.
Penny is very **careful** with her money. She doesn't spend a lot.	Sometimes, Pearl is a little **careless** with money. She spends too much.
Penny is kind of **shy**. Sometimes, she is nervous about talking to new people.	Pearl is **talkative**. She likes to meet and talk to new people.

B Penny and Pearl are sisters. Read about their personalities. Then work with a partner and answer the questions.

1. Which words in blue have a positive meaning? Which are negative?

2. Are Penny and Pearl similar or different? Why? Explain in your own words.

C Read the information note. Which sentences about Penny and Pearl use *very / really* or *kind of / a little*? Circle the words in the sentences.

> **ℹ Using Adjectives**
>
> To make adjectives stronger, use *very* or *really*.
>
> To soften adjectives, use *kind of* or *a little*.

D Complete the sentences so they are true for you. Use *very, really, kind of,* or *a little* or write *not*.

1. I'm _____ ambitious.
2. I'm _____ careful with money.
3. I'm _____ careless with money.
4. I'm _____ easy-going.

5. I'm _____ messy.
6. I'm _____ neat.
7. I'm _____ shy.
8. I'm _____ talkative.

E Are you more like Penny or Pearl? Or are you a mix? Why? Tell a partner. Use your answers in **D**.

Brothers and sisters are from the same family but can have very different personalities.

READING

LIFE STYLE

The Dreamer

A Dreamer thinks there is a "right" way to do things. This person is often hardworking, organized, and very passionate[1] about their work. Many are good listeners and want to help others. Many Dreamers work in leadership roles.

The Partner

A Partner wants to be in a group. For this person, rules are important. Tradition is important, too. Partners are often careful people, and change makes them nervous. Many do well as managers, leaders, and politicians.

The Thinker

For Thinkers, understanding things is very important. They like to solve problems and create. Thinkers can also be competitive. They like to win. They are careful, ambitious people, and they often have very strong opinions. Many Thinkers work as scientists, inventors, businesspeople, and engineers.

The Artist

Artists want to be free. They don't want to follow the rules all the time. Artists like action and are sometimes impulsive.[2] They also like to try new things, and they aren't afraid of change. Like Thinkers, many Artists have strong opinions. They do well in music, acting, the visual arts, and in some sports. 🎧63

[1] If you are **passionate** about something, you care about it a lot.
[2] An **impulsive** person does things suddenly, without thinking carefully.

A Look at the title of the reading and the four personality types. What words might describe the personality of the person in the photo?

B Guess the answers before you read. Choose **D** (*Dreamer*), **P** (*Partner*), **T** (*Thinker*), or **A** (*Artist*). Sometimes, more than one answer is possible.

This person ...

1. likes to follow the rules. **D P T A**
2. is creative. **D P T A**
3. listens to others' opinions. **D P T A**
4. tries to fix problems. **D P T A**
5. has strong opinions. **D P T A**
6. is careful. **D P T A**
7. is organized and helpful. **D P T A**
8. doesn't like change. **D P T A**
9. can be careless. **D P T A**

C Read the article and check your answers in B.

D **Personalize.** Read the article again. Which one or two of the personality types are you? Why? Tell a partner.

E Work with a new partner. Decide on one famous person for each personality type. Explain your choices to another pair of students.

"[Photographer and rock climber Jimmy Chin] is very ambitious, yet he comes across as chill . . . people really love him, want him to be successful, and want to work with him."
—Brady Robinson

LISTENING

A Read the information. How do many college students in the United States find a roommate? Tell a partner.

> In college in the United States, two students often share a small room. Many schools help students find a roommate. Students answer some questions about their personality and interests. Then the school matches them with a similar person.

B Listen. Choose the answer(s) the student chooses for questions 1–5. 🎧64

ROOMMATE QUESTIONNAIRE	

1. Which words describe you?
  a. quiet d. talkative
  b. shy e. hardworking
  c. friendly f. easy-going
	4. I like to study . . .
	  a. in the library.
	  b. in the library and the room.
	  c. mainly in my room.

2. How neat are you?
  a. I'm very neat.
  b. I'm usually neat.
  c. I'm kind of messy.
	5. Is it OK for your roommate's friends to visit your room?
	  a. Sure. I love to meet new people.
	  b. It's OK once in a while.
	  c. I don't want a lot of visitors.

3. During the week, when do you go to bed?
  a. before 11:00 p.m.
  b. 11:00 p.m.
  c. midnight or later
	6. In your free time, what do you like to do?
	  a. _____
	  b. _____
	  c. _____

C Listen again. Check your answers in **B**. Then write the three answers for the final question. 🎧64

D Read about Student A and Student B. Are they a good match as roommates? Why or why not?

Student A	Student B
I'm an energetic, friendly person. I love to make new friends and have fun. I'm hardly ever in bed before 2:00 a.m. because there's too much to do! I plan to play at least one club sport (probably soccer). I also want to do theater, so people may visit the room often to practice.	I can be kind of shy, but when you get to know me, I'm pretty funny. I'm not a messy person, but I don't clean every day. I'm usually in bed by 11:00 p.m., but sometimes, I stay up late studying. In my free time, I like to play video games or watch movies with friends once in a while.

E Complete the questionnaire in **B** for yourself. Could you and the student be roommates? Why or why not? Tell a partner.

GRAMMAR

A Read the chart. Then read the sentences below it. How are *hardly ever* and *never* different from other frequency expressions? Tell a partner.

QUESTIONS AND ANSWERS WITH *HOW OFTEN*	
How often do you clean your room?	
(I clean it)	**every** day / week / month.
	once / **twice** / **three** / **several times a** week / month.
	all the time / **once in a while**.

1. I <u>clean</u> my room **once a week**. 2. I **hardly ever** <u>clean</u> my room. 3. I **never** <u>clean</u> my room.

B Read the Unit 8, Lesson B Grammar Reference in the appendix. Complete the exercises. Then do the exercises below.

C Imagine you want to find a roommate. Read the questions and add two of your own. Then answer the questions about yourself.

How often do you . . .

1. clean your room? _____

2. stay up late? _____

3. go out with your friends? _____

4. play loud music? _____

5. _____? _____

6. _____? _____

D Take turns asking and answering the questions in **C** with a partner. Explain your answers.

E Do you and your partner have similar or different personalities? Tell the class.

“ I think we're similar. For example, we're both very neat.

I think we're kind of different. For example, . . . ”

ℹ Using *Both*
We<u>'re</u> **both** very neat.
We **both** <u>like</u> to stay up late.

F Repeat **D** and **E** with a new partner. Which person are you more similar to?

A messy room doesn't always mean someone is lazy. Many creative people have messy rooms.

48

Remember Jimmy Chin? A fun fact about him is that he can walk on a slack line.

ACTIVE ENGLISH Try it out!

A Read the fun facts. How often does / did each person do the activity. Tell a partner.

Person 1: I run ten kilometers every week.

Person 2: I volunteer at an animal shelter twice a week.

Person 3: I'm learning Italian. I listen to a podcast in Italian every night.

Person 4: I played soccer in high school. Now, I only play it once in a while.

B Think of a fun fact about yourself. Write it on a small piece of paper. Say how often you do (or did) it. Give the paper to your teacher.

C Take the paper your teacher gives you. Complete the task.

1. Read your classmate's fun fact.

2. Who wrote it? Walk around your classroom and ask.

3. When you find the person, ask two follow-up questions. Take notes.

66 Do you run ten kilometers every week?

Yes, that's me. I plan to run a half-marathon next month. 99

66 Cool. Do you go running every day?

No, I usually . . . 99

D Present the fun fact you learned about a classmate to the class. Use a personality adjective to describe the person.

E WRITING Turn to the Writing appendix. Read the student's profile. Answer the questions with a partner.

1. What adjectives does Nestor use to describe himself?

2. What are his interests?

F Answer the questions in **E** about yourself. Then use your notes and the example in the Writing appendix to write about yourself.

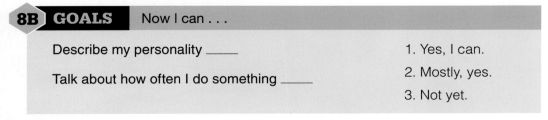

8B GOALS   Now I can . . .

Describe my personality _____

Talk about how often I do something _____

1. Yes, I can.
2. Mostly, yes.
3. Not yet.

GLOBAL VOICES

A Look at the photo and read the caption. Then look at the activities in the box. Which ones does Malaika like? Guess.

dancing   hiking   running   sailing   swimming   windsurfing

B Watch the video. Complete the sentences with the activities from **A**.

1. She likes _____. She also loves _____,
_____, and _____.

2. She doesn't enjoy _____.

3. In the future, she wants to go _____ around the world.

C Read the sentences. Then watch the video again. Choose **T** for *true* or **F** for *false*.

1. Malaika hardly ever sees marine animals when she is windsurfing.   **T   F**
2. She usually does one of the activities she likes one day a week.   **T   F**
3. She thinks she needs to work on her dancing.   **T   F**
4. She believes that going around the world sounds exciting.   **T   F**
5. She thinks she is very different from other people her age.   **T   F**

D Answer the questions in your notebook.

1. What sport or activity do you like to do? Why? How often do you do it?
2. What sport or activity don't you like? Why?
3. What sport or activity do you want to learn in the future? Why?

E Explain your answers in **D** to a partner. Do not read from your notes. Are your answers similar?

Malaika Vaz does many things—windsurfing is just one of them.

A seahorse holds onto a piece of plastic pollution near Sumbawa Island in Indonesia.

CHANGE

LOOK AT THE PHOTO. ANSWER THE QUESTIONS.

1. How do you think the plastic item got into the ocean?
2. How do human habits cause problems for the ocean?

WARM-UP VIDEO

A Look up the words *resolution* and *chore* in a dictionary. Then choose the correct answers.

1. A *resolution* is a plan to **change** / **not change** something in your life.
2. A *chore* is a **task** / **game** that you usually do in the house.

B Do you do any chores at home? Which ones? Tell a partner.

C Watch the video. Read the sentences. Choose **T** for *true* and **F** for *false*.

1. The woman does chores for 15–30 minutes each time.   **T   F**
2. She watches TV while she cleans.   **T   F**
3. She washes her clothes every day.   **T   F**
4. She deep cleans the kitchen once every couple of weeks.   **T   F**

D Watch the video again. Put the advice in the correct order.

_____ Make a schedule.

_____ Always make progress.

_____ Set realistic goals.

_____ Stay focused.

_____ Reward yourself.

E Can you think of any other advice for making changes like those in **D**? Tell a partner.

VOCABULARY

A Read about personal habits. Use a dictionary to look up any new words. Then use the questions to discuss each habit with a partner.

ℹ️ *It Depends*

You can say, "it depends" when your answer changes in different situations.

Some people **have a habit of . . .**	daydreaming.
	drinking coffee.
	eating junk food.
	napping.
	spending hours online.
	being late.

❝ | Is daydreaming a bad habit?

It depends. During class it's a bad habit because you need to pay attention. But outside of class . . . ❞

1. Is the habit a **good habit** or a **bad habit**?
2. Is the habit a **healthy** or **unhealthy habit**?

B Discuss the questions with your partner.

❝ | My sister always leaves her clothes on the floor. It really bothers me.

1. What are some good habits to have?
2. What are some healthy and unhealthy eating habits?
3. Why do you think people **fail** to **break a bad habit**?
4. How can you **build good habits**?
5. What is one small thing you can do to **make a change** in your life?
6. Always being late is an **annoying** habit that **bothers** people. What habit bothers you?

Players compete in a tournament in Chiba, Japan. The rise of eSports (electronic sports) means that more young people are spending hours online playing video games.

A to-do list is a list of tasks
(things you need to do).

LISTENING

A Read the information in the box. Do you use a to-do list?

> A to-do list is a list of tasks (things you need to do). For some people, the tasks need to be
> finished in an organized way (finished in order: first, second, third, etc.).

B **Understand context.** Listen to a two-part lecture on to-do lists. What is each part about? Choose
the best answer. 🎧65

a. Part One: the best tasks for a to-do list
    Part Two: the difficulties in making a to-do list

c. Part One: how a to-do list can help you
    Part Two: who uses a to-do list

b. Part One: the best tasks for a to-do list
    Part Two: the worst tasks for a to-do list

d. Part One: how a to-do list can help you
    Part Two: how to make a to-do list

C Read the sentences. Then listen again and complete them. 🎧65

1. You can use a to-do list to _____ your _____.

2. A to-do list can also help you to _____ good _____.

3. You _____ a task, and then you cross it off your list.

D Read each piece of advice. Then listen one more time. Write *A* if the speaker agrees with the advice
or *D* if the speaker disagrees with it. 🎧65

1. _____ Start your to-do list by writing down four or five tasks.

2. _____ Do big tasks in the afternoon.

3. _____ Make your to-do list the night before.

4. _____ Take as much time as you need for each task.

E Rewrite the sentences in **D** that the speaker disagrees with so that the speaker agrees with them.

F Work with a partner. Think of one more piece of advice for using to-do lists successfully.

SPEAKING

A Read the definitions in the Word Bank. What is a DIY project? Do you ever do these kinds of projects? Tell a partner.

B Read the conversation and listen. Then answer the questions. 🎧66

Don: Hey, Anna. How's it going? Wow! What are you doing?

Anna: I'm painting the kitchen.

Don: By yourself? That's a big project!

Anna: Yeah, but you know me—I'm in the habit of doing things myself. It saves money.

Don: Do you need any help?

Anna: Actually, there is one thing. I'd like to paint the ceiling. Can I borrow your ladder? Mine is too short.

Don: Sure. No problem.

Anna: Could you bring it tomorrow morning?

Don: I'm sorry, but I'm busy then. I can bring it in the afternoon.

Anna: Perfect! See you then.

1. What is Anna's DIY project? Why is she doing it herself?

2. How does Anna make requests? Underline your answers. How does Don respond? Circle your answers

Painting your home yourself can save a lot of money.

C Practice the conversation in **B** with a partner.

D With your partner, create your own conversation. Take turns being Student A.

1. **Student A:** Think of a DIY project. What are you doing? Why?

2. **Student B:** Ask your partner about the project.

3. **Student A:** Make two requests. Use the Speaking Strategy to help you.

4. **Student B:** Respond to the requests.

> 66 I'm putting up curtains in my new apartment.
> Really? How's it going? 99

> 66 Not great. Could I borrow your tools?
> Certainly. 99

WORD BANK
When you do a **DIY (Do It Yourself) project**, you fix or make something for the home by yourself.
in the habit of doing (something) doing something often

SPEAKING STRATEGY 🎧67
Making and Responding to Requests

Requests
Can / Could I borrow your ladder?
Can / Could you bring it tomorrow?
Positive Responses
Sure. No problem. / Of course. / Certainly.
Negative Response
I'm sorry, but . . .

GRAMMAR

A Read the chart. Choose the logical follow-up statements to Sentence 1. Underline the ones that could follow Sentence 2. Discuss your answers with a partner.

LIKE TO	WOULD LIKE TO
Sentence 1: Every summer, I **like to try** a DIY project.	Sentence 2: This summer, I'**d like to try** a DIY project.

a. I always enjoy doing it.

b. For my next one, I'm starting a garden.

c. It sounds really difficult, though.

d. It's a lot of fun.

e. People say it's a lot of fun.

B Read the Unit 9, Lesson A Grammar Reference in the appendix. Complete the exercises. Then do the exercises below.

C Read the questions. Then choose the correct words to complete each answer.

1. What do you usually do on the weekend?

   I like to / I'd like to relax.

2. Why are you studying for the TOEFL exam?

   I like to / I'd like to find a job overseas.

3. What are your goals for the new year?

   I like to / I'd like to break some bad habits.

4. What's your most unhealthy eating habit?

   I don't like to / I wouldn't like to eat breakfast.

5. How was your trip to Brazil?

   We loved it! **We like to / We'd like to** visit again.

6. Do your parents both work?

   Yes, but **they like to / they'd like to** retire soon.

D PRONUNCIATION: Contracted *Would* Listen to four sentences from **C** and repeat. Pay attention to the pronunciation of '*d*. 🎧68

E Work with a partner. Play Tic-tac-toe.

1. **Student A:** Choose any square. Make a question or statement with *like to* or *would like to*. If your answer is correct, put an *X* on that square. If your answer is incorrect, leave it blank.

2. **Student B:** Now it's your turn. Repeat Step 1, but put an *O* on the square if your answer is correct.

3. The first student with three *X*s or *O*s in a row wins.

stay up late	eat the same thing for dinner every day	speak English better
buy a new smartphone	go sightseeing with my parents	get a cat
study on the weekend	skip breakfast	go to the movies

Some people would like to eat less sugar.

ACTIVE ENGLISH Try it out!

A What would you like to do? Read the list and choose your answers. Then add three more ideas of your own.

I'd like to . . .

- eat less sugar.
- save more money.
- spend more time with friends.
- be more outgoing.
- spend less time on my phone.
- get up earlier.

- lose some weight.
- get a better job.
- be more organized.
- _____
- _____
- _____

B Choose one thing you would like to do from the list in **A**. Then ask your classmates for advice. Follow the steps.

1. You have 15 minutes. Walk around the class. Talk to as many people as you can!

2. Write down each piece of advice.

66 Could I ask you something?

66 I like to eat dessert with every meal. I'd like to eat less sugar, but it's hard to break the habit. Can you give me some advice?

Sure. 99

Of course! You can easily make a change. One idea is . . . 99

C Look at all the advice you received. Choose the three best pieces of advice.

D Work in groups. Take turns telling your classmates about your situation and the advice you received.

66 I'd like to eat less sugar, but I like sweets too much. I got some good advice. One idea was to build healthy eating habits. I can eat something sweet, like fruit, for dessert.

9A GOALS Now I can . . .

Talk about personal habits _____

Make and respond to requests _____

1. Yes, I can.
2. Mostly, yes.
3. Not yet.

VOCABULARY

A Work with a partner. Look at the photo and complete the task.

   1. Point to a **plastic** item. Use a word: *bag*, *bottle*, *cup*, *straw*.

   2. Do you ever use these things? How often?

> 66   At lunch, I usually get a drink.
> It's in a plastic cup.

B Read the information about plastic. Pay attention to the words in **blue**.
Then answer the questions with your partner.

 Every year, people put **millions** of tons of plastic in the **trash**.
It takes a long time for plastic to decompose*—450 years or more.

 Worldwide, we **recycle** very little plastic—about nine percent.
We also use some plastic items only once. We don't **reuse** them.

 Many people want to change. Their **goal** is to use less plastic.

*When things **decompose**, they break into small pieces and go away forever.

   1. What is the problem with plastic trash? Explain in your own words using the words in **blue**.

   2. After you use the items in the photo, do you put them in the trash? Do you reuse or recycle them?

   3. According to the information, what is many people's goal? Is it easy or hard to do? Why?

Many people use these plastic items once. Then they put them in the trash.

FROM **HERO** TO **ZERO**

The Start of a Bad Habit

Think about the last time you bought water, juice, or soda. It was probably in a plastic bottle. But sixty years ago, things were different. Then, most drinks—including water—were in glass bottles or aluminum cans. In many places, people could return glass bottles for a small amount of money.

Then in the 1970s, things changed. In 1973, a new kind of plastic drink bottle was invented.[1] These bottles were lighter than glass and cheap to make. Within a few years, many drinks were in plastic bottles instead of glass or aluminum. By the late 1990s, plastic water bottles were everywhere. People brought them to the gym, work or school, and on walks. "The plastic bottle transformed the beverage industry, and it changed our habits in many ways," says Dr. Peter Gleick, an expert on water issues.

Today, almost a million plastic drink bottles are sold every minute around the world. But unlike glass or aluminum, we do not recycle most of these bottles. The US, for example, recycles only 30 percent of its plastic bottles. The other 70 percent goes in the trash. In many places, these bottles fall on the ground, and then they go into the ocean. There, they pollute the water and can kill sea animals. 🎧69

[1]When something is **invented**, it is made for the first time.
[2]When something is **banned**, people cannot do or use it.
[3]We use **single-use plastic** items (shopping bags, drink bottles) one time only.

A Do you have a bottled drink with you now? Is it in a plastic bottle or a reusable bottle? Tell the class.

B **Make predictions.** Look at the photo and read the caption. Then read the title of the article and text in bold. What do you think the article is about?

C Read the article. Then complete the chart.

Period of Time	Event
In the (1.) _____	Most drinks were in glass or aluminum. People could (2.) _____ glass for (3.) _____.
In (4.) _____	A new kind of plastic drink bottle was invented.
Within a few years	Many drinks (5.) _____.
By the late (6.) _____	People brought plastic (7.) _____ bottles everywhere.
Today	(8.) _____ plastic bottles are sold every (9.) _____. We don't (10.) _____ most of these bottles.

Almost a million plastic drink bottles are sold every minute around the world.

IT'S TIME TO **CHANGE** OUR HABITS

What you can do
- Don't buy plastic bottles.
- Carry a reusable bottle.
- Recycle plastic drink bottles.

What countries are doing
- In Australia, one town banned[2] plastic water bottles completely.
- In 2019, Peru banned plastic bottles—and all other single-use plastic[3] items—from its beaches and national parks.
- Norway recycles 97 percent of its plastic bottles. The European Union has a similar goal. By 2025, it says it is going to recycle 90 percent of its plastic bottles.

D Answer the questions with a partner.

1. How did people's habits change over time? Cover **C** and explain in your own words.

2. How were plastic bottles different from glass bottles?

3. The article calls plastic bottles "a bad habit." Why?

E Work with your partner. Discuss the questions.

1. How can people use fewer plastic bottles? Do you do these things?

2. What are some countries doing? Can these actions help? Why or why not?

3. In your city or area, are people's habits changing now? Why or why not?

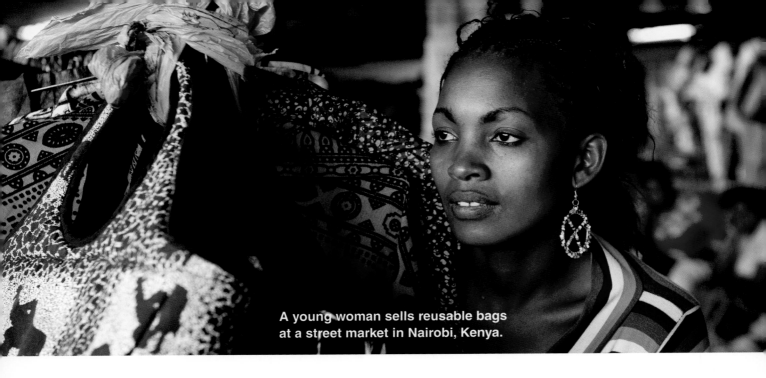

A young woman sells reusable bags
at a street market in Nairobi, Kenya.

LISTENING

A You are going to listen to an interview. Look at the photo and read the caption. What do you think the interview is about?

B Read the sentence. Then listen to the first part of an interview. Choose the correct answer. 🎧70

In 2017, Kenya banned _____ plastic bags.

a. all   b. single-use   c. reusable

C Read the sentences. Try to guess some answers. Then listen and complete 1–5. 🎧71

Before the ban	1. There were bags in the streets and in _____.
	2. Animals _____ this plastic.
	3. People used 100 _____ bags a year—just in markets.
After the ban	4. Those bags didn't become _____.
	5. Now, the streets and parks are _____.
Is the ban working?	6. _____ people follow the rule.
	7. You pay $_____ or more for using a bag.
Kenya's future goals	8. Ban _____ plastic bags.
	9. _____ more plastic.

D Listen again. Complete sentences 6–9. 🎧71

E Work with a partner. Discuss the questions.

1. Was Kenya's plastic ban a good idea? Why or why not? Use the information from **C** to explain.

2. What do you think of the ban? Why?

GRAMMAR

A Read the Unit 9, Lesson B Grammar Reference in the appendix. Complete the exercises. Then do the exercises below.

THE FUTURE WITH *BE GOING TO*					
Subject	*Be*	*(Not)*	*Going To*	Base Form	
I	am				
You	are	*not*	**going to**	buy	a reusable water bottle.
He / She	is				
We / They	are				

Yes / No and *Wh-* Questions						Answers	
	Are	you	**going to**	buy	a new bottle?	Yes, I am.	*No, I'm not.*
What	**are**	you	**going to**	buy?		(I'm going to buy) a new bottle.	
When				buy	a new bottle?	(I'm going to buy it) tomorrow.	

B Look at the list of activities. Complete the task.

1. Check (✓) three things you do and want to change.

2. What are you going to do differently? Write two sentences for each goal in your notebook.

Right now, I . . .

☐ use plastic bags when I shop.
☐ buy coffee or tea in plastic cups.
☐ use plastic straws.
☐ get takeout* in plastic boxes or cups.

☐ buy snacks in plastic packages (bags).
☐ use wrapping paper to wrap gifts.
☐ smoke cigarettes.
☐ don't recycle plastic at home.

__Takeout__ is food you buy from a restaurant and then eat in another place.

C Tell a partner your three goals. Ask and answer questions with *be going to*.

❝ I'm not going to buy snacks in plastic bags.

Are you going to stop eating snacks? ❞

❝ No, I'm going to make my own. Then I don't need a plastic bag.

Good idea! What are you going to make? ❞

D Tell the class about one of your partner's goals.

Zero-waste wrapping paper is common in Japan.

ACTIVE ENGLISH Try it out!

A Read the activities in the chart. Which ones do you do in the morning?

Activity	How does the activity use plastic?
Take a shower	Shampoo and soap are in plastic bottles.
Brush your teeth	
Shave	
Fix your hair	
Eat and drink	

WORD BANK

A **morning routine** is a list of habits. You do these things every day to start your day.

B Which activities in **A** use plastic? With your class, write them in the chart.

“ To take a shower, you use soap. The soap is in a plastic bottle.

Shampoo is in a plastic bottle, too. ”

C Work with a partner. Look at your chart in **A**. Complete the task.

You want to use less plastic in your morning routine—especially single-use plastic. How are you going to do it? For each activity in **A**, make a plan. Complete the sentences in your notebook.

i Using *Instead*

We're not going to use soap in a plastic bottle. Instead, we're going to buy . . .

1. We're not going to use _____. Instead, we are going to use _____.

2. We are going to keep using: _____ because _____.

3. Is the change going to be easy? hard? expensive? cheap? Why?

D Work with another pair of students. Complete the task. Then change roles and repeat.

Pair 1: Present your ideas from **C**.

Pair 2: Listen and take notes. At the end, tell Pair 1 which ideas you like the most.

E WRITING How are you going to use less plastic in your daily life? Turn to the Writing appendix and read one person's ideas. What is the writer going to do? What isn't the writer going to do?

F Write about your goals to use less plastic in your daily life. Use the writing example to help you.

9B GOALS	Now I can . . .	
Talk about future plans and goals _____		1. Yes, I can.
Explain a problem and how to fix it _____		2. Mostly, yes.
		3. Not yet.

GLOBAL VOICES

A Read about Melati Wijsen. Then watch Part One of the video. Complete the sentences.

Melati Wijsen is from Bali, Indonesia. As children, Melati and her sister Isabel saw a problem in their area. They decided to do something about it.

They saw (1.) _____ in the street and (2.) _____ in the water. In (3.) _____, they started an organization called Bye Bye (4.) _____.

They worked to change the (5.) _____. In 2019, Bali banned (6.) _____ plastic bags.

B Check your answers in **A** with a partner. Answer the questions.

1. What did Melati and her sister do?

2. Did things change in Bali? How long did it take?

C Read the information. Then watch Part Two of the video. Choose the correct answer(s).

The new project is called YOUTHTOPIA. Young people can join and _____.

a. talk about things they want to change   c. meet world leaders

b. learn from others   d. work with others to change the world

D Work on your own. Answer the questions in your notebook.

1. At the end of the video, Melati asks, "What changes do *you* want to see?" Think of one idea for where you live.

2. In your opinion, is the change going to happen? Why or why not?

E Work in a small group. Explain your answers in **D**. Are any of your goals the same? Tell the class about one.

Melati Wijsen (left) with her sister Isabel (right)

A Read the photo caption and the information in the box below the map. Then answer the questions.

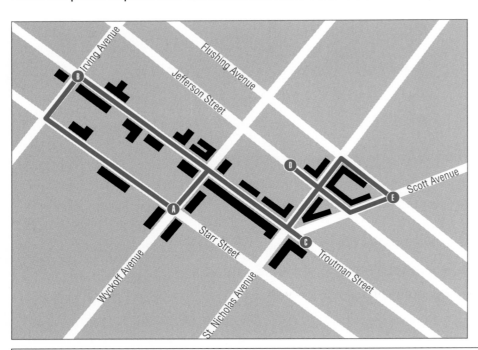

BUSHWICK ART TOUR
Use this map to do a walking tour of the murals in Bushwick.

■ = murals   ■ = walking path

1. What is Bushwick? Where is it? Why is it famous?

2. What does the map show?

3. Who is the map for?

Bushwick is a neighborhood in Brooklyn, New York City. It is famous for its murals.

B Listen to the beginning of the walking tour. Start at Point A on the map and follow along. Then listen again and choose the correct answers. 🎧72🎧

1. There are **some** / **a lot of** murals in Bushwick.

2. The walking tour takes about **one hour** / **two hours**.

3. You can see the first murals **on the corner** / **in the middle of the block**.

4. Murals in this neighborhood **hardly ever change** / **change once a year**.

5. On Starr Street, the mural is **on the right** / **in the middle of the block**.

C Work with a partner. Ask for and give directions.

Student A: Ask your partner how to get from Point B to Point C and then to Point D.

Student B: Ask your partner how to get from Point D to Point E.

D You and your partner are going to make your own walking tour. Complete the task.

1. Choose a neighborhood or area that you know well.

2. Choose a type of walking tour from the box.

3. Draw a map or use a mapmaker tool. Choose four stops (A–D) to talk about on your tour.

| **Types of Walking Tours** |
| Food |
| History |
| Shopping |
| Sports |
| your idea: _____ |

E Complete the chart. For each stop on your tour, write an interesting fact about it.

Neighborhood / Area: _____

Type of tour: _____

Stop	Why is it interesting?
A	
B	
C	
D	

F **You Choose** Using your notes in **E**, narrate the tour with your partner. Choose an option.

Option 1 Write about each stop on your map. Give directions from place to place.

Option 2 Make an audio tour. Explain each stop on the map and how to get there.

Option 3 Create a virtual tour. Show video or photos of each stop on your map. Explain each stop and how to go from place to place.

G Work with another pair of students. Look at their map and read, listen to, or watch their tour. At the end, tell them something you learned.

H Repeat **G** with two other pairs of students. Then complete the task.

1. Tell your partner about one of the tours you'd like to do. Invite your partner to join you.

2. Tell the class about a tour you're going to do.

A person relaxes in a hammock set up in a tree.

HEALTH

10

LOOK AT THE PHOTO. ANSWER THE QUESTIONS.

1. What is the person doing?
2. Is this activity good for a person's health? Why or why not?

WARM-UP VIDEO

A Read the information. Then discuss the questions with a partner.

> Therapy dogs receive special training. They can help people who have physical and mental difficulties.

1. Where are therapy dogs used?
2. Do you think therapy dogs are a good idea? Why or why not?

B Watch the video. Answer the questions.

1. Where are the therapy dogs?
2. Who is interacting with the dogs? Why?

C Watch the video again. Write the missing words.

1. People think it's normal for college students to _____ stressed out.
2. We want to rename it to Stress _____ Week.
3. This happens during finals* or other times of _____.
4. The dogs go to school two or three days a _____.
5. Students say things like, "I feel so much _____ after petting the dog."
6. Spending time with dogs can change your _____ or even your life.

*__Finals__ *are final exams that happen at the end of a course or school year.*

D Read the final sentence in **C**. Do you agree?

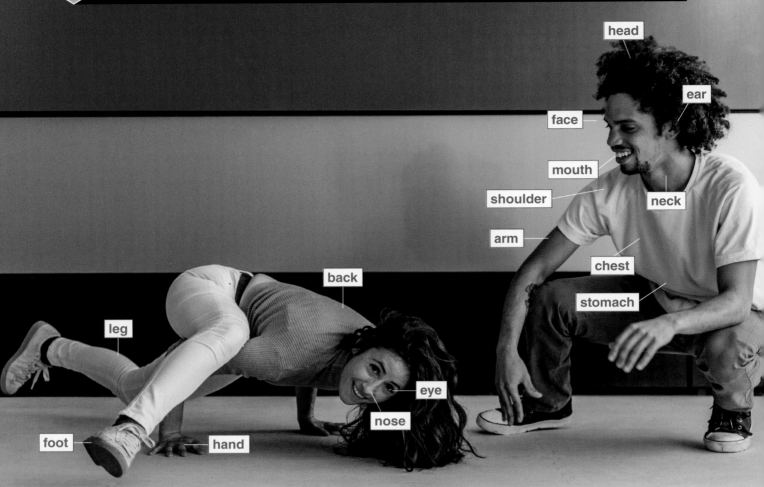

head

ear

face

mouth

shoulder

neck

arm

chest

back

stomach

leg

eye

nose

foot

hand

VOCABULARY

A Work with a partner. Look at the photo. Practice saying the words for parts of the body.

B Close your book. Can you name each part of the body without looking at the words? Tell your partner.

C Think of six actions for your partner to perform and make sentences. Use the verbs in the box and the words for the body parts.

| cover | point (to) | rub | stand (on) | touch |

D Work with your partner. Take turns telling each other your sentences from **C**.

" Cover your eyes.

Point to your left shoulder. "

WORD BANK
long ⟷ short (arms / legs)
big / large ⟷ little / small
(eyes / nose)

LISTENING

A Look at the photo and read the caption. Look up new words in a dictionary. Do you want to visit the International Space Station? Why or why not?

B Read the sentences. Then listen to the report. Choose the correct answers. 🎧73

ℹ️ NASA and SpaceX

NASA is a part of the US government. SpaceX is a private company. They both send astronauts into space.

1. How many astronauts did SpaceX send into space?

   a. two   b. three

2. Where did the astronauts go?

   a. the Moon   b. the International Space Station

3. How long did the journey take?

   a. 19 hours   b. 90 hours

4. The report is mainly about how _____ feels in space.

   a. the journey   b. the human body

C **Listen for signposts.** Listen again. Which parts of the body are mentioned? Choose your answers. Then tell a partner about the problems. 🎧73

Space Sickness   arms   back   head   legs   stomach

Muscle Problems   arms   back   head   legs   stomach

D What can astronauts do? Complete the sentences. Then listen one more time and check your answers. 🎧73

Space Sickness

1. Look at a _____ or a computer screen close by.

2. Close their _____.

Muscle Problems

3. Exercise for _____ hours every day.

4. Wear special _____ to help their _____.

The International Space Station travels around Earth. There isn't much gravity on board the space station. People can float around.

To FGB

It's important to rest when you don't feel well.

SPEAKING

A Read the conversation and listen. Answer the questions. 🎧74

Mia: Hi, Jon. It's Mia.

Jon: Mia! Where are you? I'm in front of the theater.

Mia: I'm at home.

Jon: At home? The movie starts in 15 minutes!

Mia: I know it's late, but I can't meet you tonight. I don't feel well.

Jon: Really? What's wrong?

Mia: I had a headache this afternoon. Now I have a fever,[1] and my throat hurts.

Jon: Oh, no. Sorry to hear that.

Mia: I'm really sorry.

Jon: Don't worry about it. Get some rest. I'll call you tomorrow morning.

Mia: OK. Talk to you then.

Jon: Take care.[2]

[1] A **fever** is a high body temperature.
[2] Another way to say "**take care**" is to say "be careful" or "stay healthy."

1. Where are Jon and Mia?

2. What's wrong with Mia?

3. What does Jon say?

B Work with a partner. Practice the conversation in **A**.

C PRONUNCIATION: Vowel Length Say the words. Then listen and repeat. How are the vowel sounds different? 🎧75

A	bag	phase	feed	save
B	back	face	feet	safe

D Complete the sentences with the words in the box. Then practice saying the sentences.

backache	feet	hurt	hurts	stomach

1. She has a _____. Her back hurts.

2. He has a stomachache. His _____ hurts.

3. You have a sore throat. Your throat _____.

4. I have sore _____. My feet _____.

SPEAKING STRATEGY 🎧76
Talking about Health Problems

> What's wrong? / What's the matter?
>   I don't feel well.
>   I'm sick. / I'm tired.
>   I have a fever.
>   My arm hurts.
> (I'm) sorry to hear that.

E You have plans to meet a friend, but you don't feel well. Role-play with a partner. Call your friend and explain the situation.

" I'm sorry, but I can't go to the picnic. I don't feel well.

Oh, no. What's the matter? "

GRAMMAR

A Read the Unit 10, Lesson A Grammar Reference in the appendix. Complete the exercise. Then do the exercises below.

IMPERATIVES			
Tell Someone to Do Something		**Tell Someone *Not* to Do Something**	
Stay	calm.	**Don't panic.**	
Go	straight.	**Don't turn**	right.
Close	your eyes.	**Don't move**	your arms or legs.
Take	an aspirin every day.	**Don't forget**	to do it.

B Use the verbs in the box to complete the health tips. Use affirmative or negative forms of the imperative. You will use three verbs twice.

drink	eat	give	go	sleep	take	wash

When you have a cold, there are a few things you should and shouldn't do.
(1.) _____ to school or work. (2.) _____ an
aspirin for pain and fever. (3.) _____ aspirin to children under 12!
It's dangerous. (4.) _____ a bowl of chicken soup.

When you feel better, there are a few things you can do to not get sick again.
(5.) _____ vitamins. (6.) _____ a lot of
junk food. (7.) _____ for eight to nine hours each night.
(8.) _____ your hands often. (9.) _____ a cup of
green tea daily. (10.) _____ too much soda. Water is better.

C Read the problems. Then think of another common problem and add it to the list.

1. You have a lot of homework every day. You can't sleep at night.

2. When you wake up in the morning, you're not hungry. You don't want to eat breakfast.

3. You go running twice a week. It feels good, but the next day, your legs hurt.

4. Your idea: _____

D Work with a partner. Complete the task.

1. **Student A:** Choose one of the problems from **C**. Tell your partner about it.

   Student B: Give three pieces of advice to your partner using imperatives. Start one of your sentences with *Don't*.

2. **Student A:** Choose the best piece of advice.

3. Switch roles and repeat steps 1 and 2.

66 I'm always thinking about my homework, and I can't sleep at night.

Don't study all the time. Take a break and do something fun. 99

ACTIVE ENGLISH Try it out!

A The poster gives health advice. Read it. Then answer the questions.

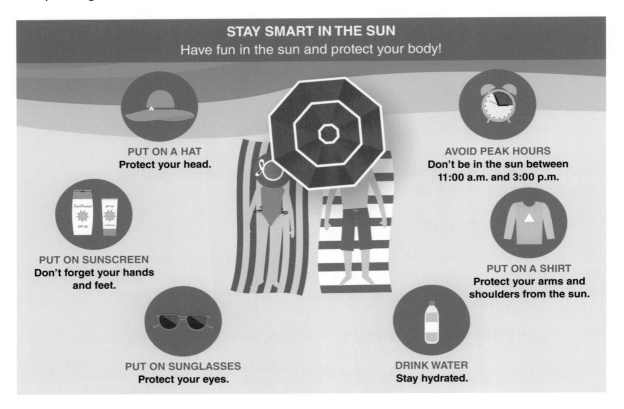

STAY SMART IN THE SUN
Have fun in the sun and protect your body!

PUT ON A HAT
Protect your head.

AVOID PEAK HOURS
Don't be in the sun between
11:00 a.m. and 3:00 p.m.

PUT ON SUNSCREEN
Don't forget your hands
and feet.

PUT ON A SHIRT
Protect your arms and
shoulders from the sun.

PUT ON SUNGLASSES
Protect your eyes.

DRINK WATER
Stay hydrated.

1. Where can you see a poster like this?

2. What does the poster tell people to do?

3. What other ideas can you add to the poster?

B Work with a partner. Read the ideas for poster titles related to health. Write another title using the imperative.

- Fight pollution in our city!
- Get in shape today!
- Eat healthy, live longer!
- Say no to smoking!
- Your idea: _____

C Work in a group. Use one of the titles from **B** to create a poster. Think of what advice to give and include it in your poster.

D With your group, work with another group. Complete the task. Then switch roles and repeat.

Group A: Present your poster to another group. Discuss it with them.

Group B: What do you like most about the other group's poster? Can you add one piece of advice to it?

10A GOALS　　Now I can . . .

Talk about health problems _____	1. Yes, I can.
Explain how to stay healthy _____	2. Mostly, yes.
	3. Not yet.

VOCABULARY

A Read the definition of **stress** in the Word Bank. What causes stress in your life? Discuss with a partner.

WORD BANK

Stress is a feeling of worry about the difficulties in your life.

B Read the sentences about stress. Choose *Agree* or *Disagree*.

1. Some people feel no stress.   Agree   Disagree
2. Stress is always bad.   Agree   Disagree
3. Stress can give you energy.   Agree   Disagree
4. Stress can make you sick.   Agree   Disagree

C Read the information. Pay attention to the words in **blue**. How are your answers in **B** similar to or different from the information?

> Everyone feels **stressed** sometimes, but not all **stressful** situations are the same. There is "good stress" and "bad stress" in our lives. When you have good stress, you feel **full of energy**. Good stress can help you **focus**. It helps you reach your goals. Good stress often **lasts** only a short time. Bad stress makes you worry. It causes **anxiety** and can even make you sick. You feel **low on energy** and want to ignore your problems.

D Read the situations and discuss the questions with a partner.

- You're planning a party for 50 people.
- You had a fight with your best friend.
- You're playing baseball. It's your turn to hit the ball.
- You're working seven days a week with no time off.
- It's your first day at a new school.

1. How long does each situation last?
2. Which situations cause the most anxiety? Which ones give you energy?

An Iranian soccer fan feels stressed watching an important game.

LESS **STRESS**
BEFORE YOUR NEXT **BIG TEST**

It's normal to be stressed before something important, like an exam.

Today is a big day: it's test day! You are nervous and don't feel well. Your stomach hurts, and your mouth is dry. Did you prepare well for your test? You think so, but you aren't sure.

Stress is normal, but there are some things you can do to reduce it. Here are some quick and easy tips to help you prepare for your next big test:

Tip One It's important to study every day before a test, but you don't want to study too much in one day. Let's say you have five days to study before your test. You remember more by studying for two hours each day than ten hours in one day—and not studying the other days.

Tip Two Studying before bed is a good idea, but don't study instead of sleeping. Go to bed when you are tired and get a good night's sleep. You can study the next day when your mind is alert.[1]

Tip Three When you sit for hours without moving, the body and mind can become tired. Get up and move around. Take a break for 10–15 minutes every hour. It can help you think more clearly.

Tip Four Don't have sugary foods or drinks when you are studying, and don't drink a lot of coffee or energy drinks. They give you energy for a short time, but then you feel tired.

Tip Five When you study for a long time, you become low on energy. To keep your energy up, eat light foods, like yogurt or nuts.

Tip Six Most of the time, you need to study alone. But you also can benefit[2] from a study partner. A partner can ask you questions to help you prepare. You can also talk to your partner to reduce stress. 🎧77

[1] An **alert** person can notice things and think quickly.
[2] When something **benefits** you, it helps you.

A Read about four students and their study habits. Are your habits similar or different? Discuss with a partner.

   a. Rachel doesn't like to eat or drink anything when she studies for a long time.

   b. Jun likes to study late at night. He drinks a lot of coffee to stay awake.

   c. There's a study group at school, but Omar isn't a member. He always studies alone.

   d. In the middle of studying, Ines stops for 15 minutes and goes for a walk.

B Read the title of the article and the first two paragraphs. Answer the questions with your partner.

   1. According to the article, how does your body feel on the day of a big test?

   2. What is one thing you think the article suggests you do to reduce stress before a big test?

C **Apply understanding.** Read the article. Which person in **A** has good study habits according to the article?

D There are six study tips in the article. Write the tip number next to the correct information.

   Tip Four Don't eat too much sugar.

   _____ Don't study after bedtime.

   _____ Study every day—don't skip days.

   _____ Don't always study by yourself.

   _____ Move around every hour.

   _____ Eat light snacks.

E Complete the study tips with follow-up information. Use your own ideas.

Don't study a lot one day.
_____

Don't study late at night.
_____

Don't sit too long without moving.
_____

Don't eat sugary foods or drink sugary drinks.
_____

Don't study alone.
_____

Some scientists believe that virtual reality (VR) can help reduce anxiety.

LISTENING

A Look at the photo. What's happening? Describe it to a partner.

B Listen to a relaxation exercise. Choose your answers. More than one answer may be possible. 🎧78

1. The relaxation exercise is for the _____.

   a. mind   b. body

2. What do you need to remember?

   a. Breathe slowly.   c. Relax one muscle group.

   b. Don't think about anything.   d. Don't try too hard.

3. How do you prepare?

   a. Look straight ahead.   c. Be quiet.

   b. Close your eyes.   d. Say, "Ready."

> **WORD BANK**
> When something is **tense**, it is tight and not relaxed.

C Listen again. Write the missing words. Then listen one more time to check your answers. 🎧78

Let's begin. (1.) _____ on your left arm. With your right hand, (2.) _____ your left arm. Rub your arm lightly. Then stop. Just (3.) _____ for a moment.

Next, bring your fingers together in your left (4.) _____. Make a fist. (5.) _____ your hand so that it feels tight. Hold the fist for five to seven seconds. Then let go. Just (6.) _____ your arm.

How does your left arm and hand feel? This is the most important part. Notice the (7.) _____.

D Complete the task.

1. Read the text in **C** silently to yourself.

2. Take turns reading the text to a partner.

   Student A: Read the text. Give your partner instructions for their *right* arm.

   Student B: Close your eyes. Listen to **Student A**.

3. Switch roles and do it again. How do you feel after doing the exercise?

GRAMMAR

A Read the Unit 10, Lesson B Grammar Reference in the appendix. Complete the exercises. Then do the exercises below.

WHEN CLAUSES	
When Clause	Result Clause
When(ever) I drink coffee,	I can't sleep.
Result Clause	*When* Clause
I can't sleep	when(ever) I drink coffee.

B Complete the sentences for yourself. Don't show anyone else your answers.

1. When I have a headache, I take _____.

2. I eat _____ when my stomach hurts.

3. Don't drink _____ when you can't sleep.

4. When I can't focus on my homework, I _____.

5. I feel _____ when I speak in English.

6. When I have a lot to do, I feel _____.

7. When the weekend comes, I am _____ energy.

C Work with a partner. Complete the task. How similar are you?

1. Read the first sentence in **B** aloud and stop before your answer.

2. Count down: "3, 2, 1."

3. After you say "1," say the word(s) you wrote at the same time.

4. Score one point if you and your partner say the same thing.

5. Repeat steps 1–4 for the other sentences in **B**. How many words did you match?

D Take turns reading your completed sentences in **B** to your partner. Give additional information.

> ❝ When I feel stressed, I go outside and exercise.

A mountain biker enjoys a bike trail in Washington State, US.

A man enjoys Renmin Park in Chengdu, China. Spending time in nature can help combat stress.

ACTIVE ENGLISH Try it out!

A How stressed are you? Choose *Yes* or *No*. Compare your answers with a partner.

1. I often feel stressed.   Yes   No
2. When I get tired, it's hard to focus.   Yes   No
3. I'm often low on energy.   Yes   No
4. My homework is stressful.   Yes   No

B What can you do to relax? Read the list. Add at least two of your own ideas to the list.

Listen to relaxing music.

Take a hot bath.

Go for a walk.

Watch a funny video.

C Make a plan to have less stress in your life. Complete the task.

1. Make a list of your daily activities.
2. Give each activity a number (1 = very stressful, 2 = a little stressful, 3 = not stressful).
3. Cross out one of the very stressful activities and write in a relaxing activity.

D Share your idea from **C** with a partner.

E **WRITING** Write about your own experience with stress. Turn to the Writing appendix to see an example. Then answer the questions. Use your answers to write about your own experience.

1. What makes you stressed? How does it make you feel?
2. What do you do to feel better?

10B GOALS   Now I can . . .

Describe stress and its causes _____

Talk about how to have less stress _____

1. Yes, I can.
2. Mostly, yes.
3. Not yet.

GLOBAL VOICES

A What is one way you deal with stress? Tell a partner.

B In the video, some friends talk about stress. Guess the answers. Then watch the video and complete the sentences.

1. Lots of different things can cause _____.

2. My name is JY, and I'm a _____.

3. My name is Lara, and I'm from _____.

4. How much stress do you have in your _____?

5. How much is related to your _____?

6. What do you do to relieve _____?

C What do JY and Lara say about stress? Match each sentence to the correct person.

1. I have an anxious personality.

2. I get a lot of stress from work.   JY

3. I have two dogs.

4. I just hold stress in.

5. I eat away my stress.   Lara

6. I go to cafes with dogs.

D Look at the list in **C**. Are you similar to JY or Lara in any way? Tell a partner.

Cat cafes, like this one in Tokyo, Japan, are very popular with stressed students.

ACHIEVEMENT

LOOK AT THE PHOTO. ANSWER THE QUESTIONS.

1. What are the girls doing? Why?

2. How do you think they feel? Why?

WARM-UP VIDEO

A Read the information. Then answer the questions with a partner.

> Caine is a nine-year-old boy. His father works at a car repair shop, and Caine spent his summer vacation there. Caine had a lot of free time, so he decided to use old boxes to make an arcade.* There was only one problem: not many people came to the repair shop, so Caine didn't have any customers.

*An **arcade** is a place where people play games for prizes.

1. Who is Caine?

2. What did he make?

3. What's his problem?

B Watch the video. Choose the correct words to complete the sentences.

1. Caine's first game was a **basketball** / **soccer** game.

2. Nirvan learned about Caine's Arcade when he **saw it online** / **went to the repair shop**.

3. To play arcade games, it costs one dollar for four turns or two dollars for **5** / **500** turns.

4. Nirvan made a plan to invite **a few friends** / **everyone in the city** to Caine's arcade.

5. When Caine saw the people, he was very **worried** / **excited**.

C Work with a partner. Answer the questions.

1. Why do you think Nirvan helped Caine?

2. What do you think of Caine and his idea?

An ice skating team from Finland celebrates winning a championship in England, UK.

GOALS

Lesson A

/ Talk about past and present abilities

/ Give and respond to compliments

Lesson B

/ Talk about taking risks

/ Give reasons and explain results

VOCABULARY

A Say the words in the chart with your teacher. Which ones do you know? Look up any new words in a dictionary.

Word Families: *Success* and *Talent*		
Noun	**Verb**	**Adjective**
success	succeed	successful
talent		talented

B Read about Hou Yifan. Complete the text with words from the chart in **A**. Use one word twice.

Everyone has a (1.) t _____—something they can do well. A person can be **good at** math, a sport, or playing a musical instrument. But some people, like Hou Yifan, have a **special ability**. As a child, Yifan was already a (2.) t _____ chess player. By age 14, she was a Grandmaster—the highest title that a chess player can achieve.

Why was Yifan so (3.) s _____? Was it a natural (4.) t _____? Did she study the game and **practice** a lot? Or did she (5.) s _____ for another reason?

Hou Yifan achieved the highest title in chess when she was just 14 years old.

C Check your answers in **B** with a partner. Then ask and answer the questions.

1. What is Hou Yifan good at?
2. What special title did she get when she was 14?
3. In your opinion, why is she so successful?

D Think of a talented person. It can be someone famous or someone you know. Answer the questions in your notebook.

1. Who is the person?
2. What is the person good at?
3. How often does the person practice or do the activity?
4. Is the person successful because of their talent?

E Tell a partner about your person in **D**. Are your two people similar in any way? Why or why not?

" My uncle is really good at fixing old cars. He's an amazing mechanic! He has his own shop and is very successful.

My sister has her own business, too. "

LISTENING

A Look at the photo and read the caption. Do you know anything about Pablo Picasso? Tell a partner.

WORD BANK
genius a very talented or intelligent person

B You are going to listen to two people talk about Picasso. Guess the answers to complete the sentences. Then listen and check your ideas. 🎧79

Picasso was a very (1.) _____ painter. Picasso also (2.) _____ things differently—he (3.) _____ different styles of painting and drawing. His ideas (4.) _____ the art world.

C Why else was Picasso successful? Listen and choose three reasons. 🎧80

1. He had money.   4. He worked hard.
2. He had goals.   5. He had good friends.
3. He was handsome.   6. He loved his work.

D **Test comprehension.** Work with a partner. Complete the tasks.

1. Choose the sentence that the man would agree with. Use your answers in **B** and **C** to explain.

   a. To be successful in life, talent is the most important.

   b. To be successful in life, you need more than talent.

2. Do you agree with the man's opinion? Why or why not?

Many people believe Spanish painter Pablo Picasso was a genius.

Are you good at making a special dish? Can you explain how to make it?

SPEAKING

A Read the conversation and listen. Then answer the questions. 🎧81

Victor: Hey, Ayumi. Are you enjoying the party?

Ayumi: I am. Thanks for inviting me.

Victor: Sure. Are you hungry? There's a lot of food.

Ayumi: I just tried one of these little dumplings. What's it called?

Victor: It's called *pierogi*.

Ayumi: Did you make them?

Victor: I did.

Ayumi: They're really good. You're a great cook.

Victor: Thanks. That's nice of you to say.

Ayumi: Are pierogi easy to make?

Victor: Yeah, really easy. I can teach you.

1. What nice things does Ayumi say to Victor? Underline the sentences.

2. What is Victor's reply? Circle it.

3. What follow-up question does Ayumi ask?

B Practice the conversation in **A** with a partner.

C Practice the conversation in **A** again. Use a different expression to compliment. Ask a different follow-up question, too.

D Use the situations to make two new conversations with your partner. In each conversation, give a compliment and ask a follow-up question. Then do one role play for another pair of students.

SPEAKING STRATEGY 🎧82
Complimenting Someone on Ability

Compliment	Reply
Great / Good job!	
This food is amazing / really good.	Thanks.
You're a great cook.	Thank you.
I like this food a lot.	That's nice of you to say.
You can cook really well.	

Situation 1
Student A: You play the guitar. You wrote a new song, and you're practicing it.
Student B: You think your partner plays well and is really talented.

Situation 2
Student A: You gave a presentation in English to the class today.
Student B: You think your classmate's presentation was very good.

GRAMMAR

A Read the Unit 11, Lesson A Grammar Reference in the appendix. Complete the exercises. Then do the exercises below.

CAN AND COULD FOR ABILITY			
Subject	Modal Verb	Base Form	
I / You / He / She / We / They	**can** / can't **could** / couldn't	cook	well.

QUESTIONS AND SHORT ANSWERS			
Can	you	cook well?	Yes, I can. / No, I can't.
	he		Yes, he can. / No, he can't.
Could	you	cook well at age 16?	Yes, I could. / No, I couldn't.
	he		Yes, he could. / No, he couldn't.

B PRONUNCIATION: *Can / Can't, Could / Couldn't* Listen and write *can*, *can't*, *could*, or *couldn't*. 🎧83

1. I _____ play the guitar.

2. I _____ play the piano.

3. **A:** _____ you play music?
   B: I _____.

4. She _____ play chess as a child.

5. I _____ play chess as a child.

6. **A:** _____ you play chess as a child?
   B: I _____, but my brother _____.

C Listen again and say the sentences in **B**. Then practice saying them with a partner. 🎧83

D Work with a new partner. Complete the task.

Student A: Turn to the Information Gap Activities appendix. Follow the directions there.

Student B: Look at the chart. You want to learn about Ana. Ask your partner questions with *can* and *could*. Put a (✔) for *yes* or an (✗) for *no*.

	Leo (Now)	Leo (3 years ago)	Ana (Now)	Ana (3 years ago)	✔ = yes ✗ = no
Speak English	✔	✔	✔		
Cook well	✗	✗			
Ride a bike	✔	✗			
Dance	✗	✗			
Stay up late	✔	✔			

❝ Can Ana speak English now?

Yes, she can. ❞

❝ Could she speak it three years ago?

E Now answer your partner's questions about Leo. Use the information in the chart. Give short answers with *can*, *can't*, *could*, or *couldn't*.

F Can your partner do any of the activities from the chart in **D** now? How about in the past? Take turns asking questions.

ACTIVE ENGLISH Try it out!

A Read about the TV show *Talent Search!* Do you know shows like this one?

> *Talent Search!* is a popular TV show. Talented people go on the show and try to win prizes. Some people sing, dance, or play an instrument. Others tell jokes, do magic tricks, or draw a picture.

B Imagine that you are going to be on *Talent Search!* Answer the questions in your notebook.

1. What is something you're good at?
2. How did you learn to do it?
3. Could you do it when you were young?
4. What are you going to do on the talent show?

C Work with a partner. Ask the questions in **B**. Take notes.

" What's something you're good at?

I can . . . "

" That's amazing! How did you learn to do that?

I practiced every day for six months. At first, I couldn't do it at all, but then . . . "

D Join two other pairs of students. With your partner, complete the task.

" Here's a talented young woman from Lima, Peru—Maria! She can . . .

1. **Student A:** You are a *Talent Search!* announcer. Introduce your partner to the group. Use your notes from **C**.

   Student B: What is your talent? Do it for the group. If you can't do it, explain it or show a photo.

   I can't cook for you now, but I can show you some photos. "

2. **Listeners:** Compliment the person on their ability.

3. Repeat steps 1 and 2 with another pair of students.

" Wow, that food looks amazing!

E Tell the class about one person in your group.

Thanks! "

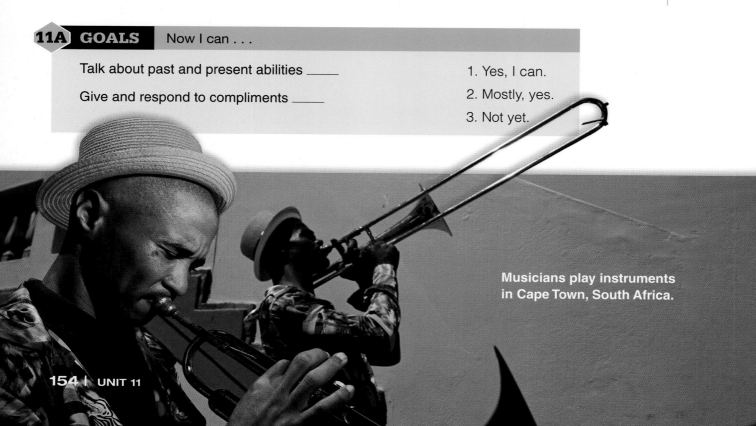

11A GOALS Now I can . . .

Talk about past and present abilities _____

Give and respond to compliments _____

1. Yes, I can.
2. Mostly, yes.
3. Not yet.

Musicians play instruments in Cape Town, South Africa.

VOCABULARY

A Look at the photo. What is the man doing? What words can you use to describe the person?

WORD BANK
brave ↔ afraid
dangerous ↔ safe
difficult ↔ easy

B Read the description of a risk-taker. Pay attention to the words in blue. Then choose your answers. Explain your ideas to a partner.

> Risk-takers are **brave** people. They aren't **afraid** to try **dangerous** or **difficult** things, like walking on a wire. They are **curious**. They like to ask questions and learn new things. They aren't afraid of making mistakes. They might start their own company, for example. It might succeed or it might fail, but risk-takers still **take a chance** and try.

A risk-taker might . . .

1. move to another country.
2. talk to a new person at a party.
3. do the same job all his or her life.
4. do the activity in the photo.

C Choose the answers so the sentences are true for you.

1. Usually, I **am** / **am not** afraid to take a chance and try new things.
2. The activity in the photo looks **very dangerous** / **kind of fun**.
3. When something is difficult, I usually **stop doing it** / **try harder**.
4. I **am** / **am not** curious about other countries and cultures.

D Tell a partner your answers to the questions in **C**. Are you a risk-taker?

A group of people watch their friend walk on a wire in Yosemite National Park, California, US.

A BRAVE
PILOT

Barrington Irving with his plane

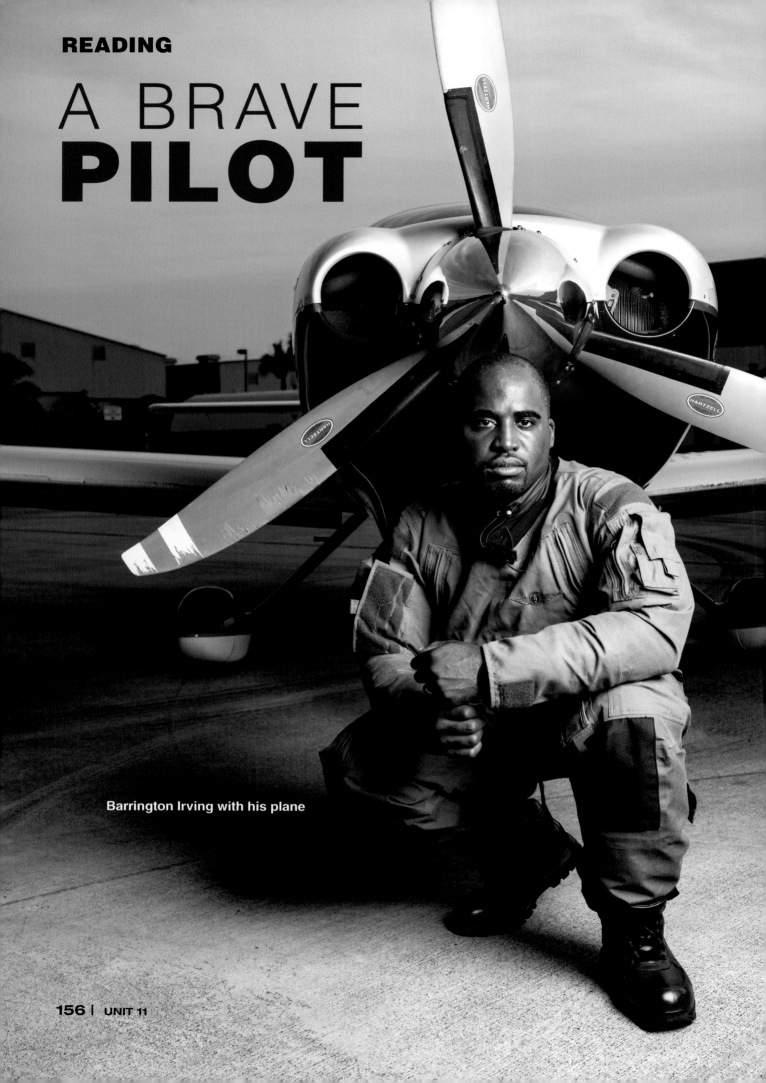

1 At age 23, Barrington Irving became the youngest person to fly alone around the world—in a small plane he built himself. Since then, he started a company called Experience
5 Aviation. It helps curious[1] students learn about flying and other subjects, like science and math. Students can study in the "Flying Classroom" or learn how to build cars.

Here, Barrington Irving talks about his love of
10 flying and his flight around the world.

Why do you fly?

I love being in the air between the sky and the earth. It's exciting, but I also feel very calm.

Are you ever afraid?

15 Yes, I was very afraid one time. It was during my flight around the world. I had to fly from Japan to a small island called Shemya, near Alaska. The flight was difficult. It was very windy, and then there was a bad storm. At
20 one point, the team on the ground sent me a message. They said, "You have to go back to Japan." And I said, "I don't have enough fuel[2] to go back." It wasn't safe to continue, but I had to keep going. The team asked for my
25 parents' phone number. It was the end for me, they thought, but I didn't give up. When I got to Shemya Island, I had 12 minutes of fuel left.

What a frightening experience!

30 Yes, it was, but I got to Shemya safely. I made it. And I learned a lot from the experience. 🎧84

[1] A **curious** person wants to learn about new things.
[2] **Fuel** is another word for "gas."

A Look at the photo. Read the title and the first sentence in the first paragraph. Then answer the questions.

1. What is Barrington Irving's job?

2. He did something dangerous. What was it? Was the experience difficult? Guess.

B Read the rest of the article. Choose the correct answers. Underline the information that helped you choose your answers.

1. Irving flies because _____.
   a. it's a good job
   b. he likes the feeling of flying

2. Irving's trip from Japan to Shemya was dangerous because _____.
   a. the weather was bad
   b. he didn't have enough time

3. Irving didn't go back to Japan because _____.
   a. he didn't have enough gas
   b. his plane stopped

4. The team asked for Irving's parents' phone number because they _____.
   a. wanted to help Irving
   b. thought Irving might die

5. Irving says the experience _____.
   a. taught him a lot
   b. was exciting

C Choose the correct answer in each sentence.

1. In line 26, *give up* means . . .
   continue / quit / talk.

2. In line 29, *frightening* means . . .
   hard / exciting / scary.

3. In line 30, Irving says, "I made it." This means, "I did something . . .
   successfully / poorly / slowly."

D Apply ideas. Answer the questions.

1. Irving says he learned a lot from his difficult trip. What do you think he learned?

2. How can difficult experiences help us learn?

LISTENING

A   Listen to the first part of the speaker's story. Choose two answers to the question.   85

What difficult thing happened to the speaker when he was fifteen?

   a. His family moved to a new place.   c. He lost a part-time job.

   b. He failed a class at school.   d. He didn't have friends.

B   Listen to the second part of the speaker's story. Put the events in order from 1–6.   86

   1. _____ He joined the group.

   2. _____ His playing got better.

   3. __1__ He saw a poster for the school jazz band.

   4. _____ He made friends.

   5. _____ He practiced the piano every day.

   6. _____ He went to the first meeting.

C   What did the speaker learn from his experience? Listen. Then complete the sentences.   87

My family had to (1.) _____ because my dad got a new (2.) _____.
I couldn't change that, but I (3.) _____ do something to be
(4.) _____. So, I took a chance and joined the school band. Then
I made (5.) _____.

When I started with the jazz band, I had to (6.) _____ a lot. I learned that
it takes (7.) _____ to do something well. So even now, when something
is (8.) _____, I don't (9.) _____ up right away.

D   Listen again and check your answers in **C**.   87

E   Work with a partner. Cover your answers in **A–C**. Take turns retelling the speaker's story in one minute or less. Use the questions to help you.

   1. What happened to the speaker?

   2. Did things get better? Why or why not?

   3. What did the speaker learn from the experience?

F   Think about a difficult experience that you or someone you know had. Use one of the topics in the box or your own idea. Answer the questions in **E**. Then tell your partner about the experience.

> **Topics**
> Moving
> Starting a new school or job
> Taking an important exam
> My idea: _____

GRAMMAR

A Read the Unit 11, Lesson B Grammar Reference in the appendix. Complete the exercises. Then do the exercises below.

CONNECTING IDEAS WITH *BECAUSE*	
Main Clause	**Reason Clause**
My family moved	**because** my dad got a new job.
Reason Clause	**Main Clause**
Because my dad got a new job,	my family moved.

CONNECTING IDEAS WITH *SO*	
Main Clause	**Result Clause**
My dad got a new job,	**so** my family moved.

B Work in a small group. Play the game.

1. Write the sentence pairs from the box on four small pieces of paper. Mix them and put them face down on the desk.

2. On three small pieces of paper, write the word *so*. On another three, write *because*. Mix these and put them face down in another pile.

3. One person begins. Turn over a word (*so* or *because*) and one of the sentence pairs. You have ten seconds to join the two sentences. If you do this correctly, you get a point.

4. When you are done, put the two pieces of paper back. Then the next person goes.

5. Play the game for 15 minutes. The person with the most points wins.

> 1. I'm taking an English class.
>   I need English for my job.
> 2. I don't smoke.
>   Smoking is dangerous.
> 3. I'm saving my money.
>   I want to travel.
> 4. I want to change my major.
>   It's boring.

66 | I need English for my job, so . . .

C Are any of the sentences from the game in **B** true for you? Why or why not? Tell a partner.

66 | I'm saving my money because I want to travel to Brazil.

Why do you want to go to Brazil? 99

66 | Because it's an interesting country.

A couple looks at Sugar Loaf Mountain in Rio de Janeiro, Brazil.

ACTIVE ENGLISH Try it out!

WORD BANK
A **bucket list** is a list of things you want to do in your life.

A Read the definition of a bucket list. Then look at the list of activities. Complete the task.

- ☐ Go the World Cup
- ☐ Visit another country
- ☐ Start your own business
- ☐ Learn to play music

- ☐ Be on a reality TV show
- ☐ Get a tattoo
- ☐ Get married
- ☐ Go skydiving

- ☐ Get an advanced degree
- ☐ Buy a house
- ☐ _____
- ☐ _____

1. Which activities do you want to do? Check (✔) them.
2. Which activities do you not want to do? Put an *X* next to them.
3. Think of two more activities and add them to the list.

B Tell a partner your answers in **A**. Explain each one with *because* or *so*. Your partner will ask you questions.

“ I don't want to learn to play music.

Why? ”

“ Because I can play the piano and cello already.

Wow, you're really talented! ”

C What is one of your goals? Why do you want to do it? Tell the class.

D **WRITING** What is something you want to do in the future? Turn to the Writing appendix to see an example of one person's answer. What is the writer's goal? Why do they want to do this?

E Answer the question in **D** about yourself. Use one of your answers from **A** and the writing example to help you.

11B GOALS Now I can . . .

Talk about taking risks _____

Give reasons and explain results _____

1. Yes, I can.
2. Mostly, yes.
3. Not yet.

GLOBAL VOICES

A Read about the three National Geographic Explorers. Look up any new words in a dictionary.

Archana Anand	
1. What is your proudest accomplishment? a. She worked in the ocean. b. She worked near her hometown. c. She worked with children.	**2.** Why are you happy about it? People take the ideas _____. a. home b. to Vietnam c. to the ocean
Debby Ng	
3. What is your proudest accomplishment? a. She became a successful doctor. b. She is a role model for girls. c. She saved an animal's life.	**4.** Why are you happy about it? In rural places, seeing _____ doctors is rare. a. young b. foreign c. female
Ruchira Somaweera	
5. What is your proudest accomplishment? a. He's changing people's minds about reptiles. b. He's teaching people about a special snake. c. He found a new kind of reptile.	**6.** Why are you happy about it? It can save _____. a. money b. lives c. time

B Watch the video. Choose the correct answers in **A**.

C Watch the video again and check your answers in **A**.

D What is your proudest accomplishment? Why?

E Work with a partner. Complete the task.

    1. Ask your partner the question in **D**. Listen to their answer.

    2. Compliment your partner and ask a follow-up question.

WORD BANK

ladies women

misunderstood not understood

mindset / viewpoint how you think about something

proudest accomplishment something you did successfully and feel good about

Ruchira Somaweera studies reptiles like crocodiles.

People watch a movie at a floating movie theater in Paris, France.

GOALS

AT THE MOVIES

LOOK AT THE PHOTO. ANSWER THE QUESTIONS.

1. What are the people doing?
2. What type of movie are the people watching?

WARM-UP VIDEO

A The video is about the Patricia Theater. Read the sentences. Then watch the video and choose your answers.

1. Ann Nelson _____ the movie theater.

    a. sold   b. owns

2. The Patricia Theater is in _____.

    a. a large Canadian city

    b. a town that is far from other places

3. The Patricia Theater is *a social hub*. This means it's a place for people to _____.

    a. get together and have fun

    b. learn to act in the movies

4. Ann says it's fun to watch movies in _____.

    a. a theater   b. your living room

B Watch the video again and check your answers in **A**.

C Work with a partner. Answer the questions.

1. Is the Patricia Theater important? Why or why not?

2. Do you agree with Ann's opinion in the final sentence in **A**?

VOCABULARY

A Look at the types of movies in **blue**. Complete the task.

1. Say the types of movies with your teacher.

2. Look at the movie poster. What type of movie is *Science Fair*?
    What is it about? Was it a successful movie? How do you know?

**The documentary *Science Fair* follows nine
high school students from around the world as
they try to win an important science contest.**

Types of Movies

_____ 1. **action movie**

_____ 2. **classic movie**

_____ 3. **documentary**

_____ 4. **drama**

_____ 5. **horror movie**

_____ 6. **romantic comedy**

_____ 7. **science fiction (sci-fi)**

Movie Titles

a. *My Neighbor Totoro (1988)*

b. *Fright Night*

c. *James Bond: No Time to Die*

d. *Lost in Space*

e. *Love, Rosie*

f. *Science Fair*

g. *The Farewell (A tearful goodbye)*

B Work with a partner. Complete the task.

1. Match each movie title in **A** with a type of movie. Discuss
    your answers as a class.

2. What types of movies make you laugh, feel afraid, think, and
    feel good?

❝❞ A comedy makes
you laugh.

C Answer the questions with your partner.

1. Which types of movies do you like? Which types of movies
    don't you like? Why?

2. What was the last movie you saw? What type
    of movie was it? Did you like it? Why or why not?

❝❞ I saw . . . Did you
see it?

Yeah, I
saw it. ❞

❝❞ I thought it was
great!

D For each type of movie in **A**, write another movie in your notebook.

Fans of the movie *Twilight* camp outside a movie theater in Los Angeles, California to be the first people to see the movie.

LISTENING

A The words (1–4) describe movies. What do they mean? Guess and match. Then check your answers with the class.

1. animated movie   a. a big, successful movie that many people see
2. biopic   b. a movie that is made on computers
3. blockbuster   c. a movie that continues a story
4. sequel   d. a drama about a real person's life

B **Listen for signposts.** Read the information note. Then listen. Check (✓) the movie each person likes. 🎧88

	The woman likes…	The man likes…
1. the biopic	☐	☐
2. action movies	☐	☐
3. the Spider-Man movie	☐	☐
4. *A Quiet Place, Part One*	☐	☐
5. the animated movie	☐	☐

> **ℹ Talking About Likes and Dislikes**
>
> I'm (not) into . . .
> I'm (not) a big fan of . . .

C Listen again. Then write the correct letters (a–f). 🎧88

a. the animated movie	c. the James Bond movie	e. the sci-fi sequel
b. the biopic	d. the sci-fi movie (Part One)	f. the Spider-Man movie

Which movie . . .

1. is about a real person? _____
2. did the man see recently? _____
3. is really popular this summer? _____
4. has very little talking in it? _____
5. is about two teenagers? _____
6. do the speakers watch? _____

D Look again at the words to describe movies in **A** (1–4). Write a movie for each one in your notebook. Do you like these movies?

Sometimes, it's hard to hear people on the phone in busy places, like this subway station in Tokyo, Japan.

SPEAKING

A Read the conversation and listen. Write the times. 🎧89

Marc: Hello?

Isabel: Marc? Hi, it's Isabel.

Marc: Hey! How's it going?

Isabel: Good. Where are you? It's really noisy.

Marc: I'm at the subway station.

Isabel: Oh, OK. Listen—change of plans. We're meeting at the movie theater tonight at _____.

Marc: Sorry, I didn't catch that. Can you say that again? *What* time?

Isabel: We're meeting at the theater at _____, not _____.

Marc: Got it.

Isabel: I tried to text you earlier, but you didn't answer.

Marc: Oh, sorry about that.

Isabel: No problem. See you soon.

Marc: OK, bye.

B Listen again. Then answer the questions. 🎧89

1. What plan changed?

2. How do Marc and Isabel start the phone conversation? How do they end it?

3. At one point, Marc doesn't hear Isabel. What does he say?

C Practice the conversation in **A** with a partner.

D Work with a new partner. Imagine that you are going to see a movie. Complete the information.

Movie Name: _____

Where: _____

Movie Time: _____

Time to Meet: _____

E Work on your own. Change <u>two</u> pieces of information in **D**. Do not show your partner.

F Sit back to back with your partner. Imagine you are talking on the phone. Complete the task.

1. **Student A:** Call your partner. Explain the change of plans.
   Student B: Talk to your partner. Make notes about the change of plans.

2. Change roles. Repeat Step 1.

SPEAKING STRATEGY 🎧90
Talking on the Phone

Starting a Phone Call	A: Hello? B: Hi. It's . . .
Ending a Phone Call	See you (later / soon). / Bye.
Asking Someone to Repeat	(Sorry,) I didn't hear you. Can you repeat that? (Sorry,) I didn't catch that. Can you say that again?

GRAMMAR

A Read the Unit 12, Lesson A Grammar Reference in the appendix.
Complete the exercises. Then do the exercises below.

THE PRESENT CONTINUOUS AS FUTURE			
Subject + *Be*	Verb + *-ing*		Future Time Expression
We're	meeting	at the theater	at 8:00. in an hour. today / tonight / tomorrow.
I'm	going	to a movie	this weekend.
They're	releasing	the sequel	next year.

B Choose three more correct sentences. Check your answers with a partner.

1. We're seeing a movie later today.
2. I'm meeting them at the movie theater at two o'clock.
3. We're having a lot of snow next week.
4. They're watching the Oscars tonight.
5. You need to rest or you're getting sick.
6. I'm studying for a test after school.

C PRONUNCIATION: Sentence Stress Read the information note.
Then listen to the sentence. 🎧91

We're <u>seeing</u>   a <u>movie</u>   <u>later today</u>.
   main verb   noun   time expression

i **Content Words**

In a sentence, content words give us the most important information. We say them with more stress.

D Look at the three sentences you chose in **B**. Underline the content words.
Then listen and repeat the sentences. 🎧92

E Work with a partner. Look again at the sentences you chose in **B**. Use
them to make a short conversation.

The Oscars is a movie
awards shows in the US.
Do you ever watch this
show? Which movies
won awards last year?

The Hindi film industry, also known as Bollywood, is based in Mumbai, India. It makes close to 1,000 movies every year.

ACTIVE ENGLISH Try it out!

A Work with a partner. You are going to create a poster for a new movie. Complete the task.

1. Write the names of two actors in your movie.

   _____   _____

2. Choose one of the following to appear in your movie.

   a monster   a superhero   a talking animal

   an alien   a spy   your idea: _____

3. Choose a location for your movie: _____

4. What type of movie is it? Choose one.

   action   documentary   drama   horror

   animation   romantic comedy   sci-fi   other: _____

5. Finally, think of a title for your movie: _____

B Now make a poster advertising your movie. Then put it on the classroom wall.

C Walk around the classroom and look at the posters. Which movie do you want to see? Choose one.

D Work with a partner. Role-play a conversation on the phone.

1. **Student A:** Call and invite your partner to see your movie choice from **C**. Say when you are going.

2. **Student B:** Respond to the invitation. If you say *no*, explain why.

3. Change roles and repeat steps 1 and 2.

     ❝ Hello?

     Emilio? Hi! It's Anita. ❞

     ❝ Hey! How's it going?

     Good. Listen, I'm seeing . . . with two classmates tonight. Do you want to come? ❞

     ❝ Sure! What time are you going?

12A GOALS   Now I can . . .

Describe types of movies _____

Talk about and make future plans _____

1. Yes, I can.

2. Mostly, yes.

3. Not yet.

VOCABULARY

A Use the words in the box to complete the opinions.

boring	entertaining	funny	original	scary	surprising	violent

1. My parents like classic movies, but I think they're _____. I usually fall asleep when they're on.

2. I like sweet and happy movies that are _____ for the whole family. Everyone has a good time.

3. I like horror movies, but I cover my eyes during the _____ parts.

4. When the _____ movie is good, I want to see the sequel. Usually, though, the sequel is not as good.

5. Action movies are **exciting**, but a lot of them are _____.

6. I like _____ movie **characters**. They make me laugh.

7. The best movies always have a _____ (and unexpected) ending.

B Read the opinions in **A** again. Are your experiences with movies the same or different? Tell a partner. Explain why.

> " I don't think classic movies are boring. The stories are usually entertaining, and the acting is good.

C Work with a new partner. Complete the task.

1. **Student A:** Complete the sentence with one of the words. Read the sentence to your partner.

   Name a(n) _____ *movie.*

   a. boring   c. exciting   e. scary

   b. entertaining   d. funny   f. violent

   Student B: Say a movie. Then tell your partner about it in one or two sentences.

2. Continue until all the words are used. Then switch roles and repeat Step 1.

A group of friends dress up to watch *Black Panther* in 3-D at a movie theater in Nairobi, Kenya.

A MOVIE REMAKE

Shutter[1] (Original)

In this popular movie from Thailand, Tun, a photographer, and his girlfriend, Jane, are driving home on a dark country road one night. Suddenly, they see a girl in the road. Jane tries to stop the car, but it's too late. She hits and kills the girl. Tun and Jane are scared. They stay in the car. Then they leave the girl and quickly drive back home to Bangkok. Jane and Tun try to return to normal life, but strange things start happening. Tun starts to have bad neck pain. Both Jane and Tun see strange images in Tun's photographs. They look like a girl. Is it the girl from the road?

Shutter (Remake)

The main characters are Jane and her husband, Ben. They move to Tokyo for Ben's new job as a photographer. One night, they are in a car accident on a country road. They hit a young girl and also hit a tree. When they wake up, they look for the girl, but they can't find her. Was the girl really there? They return to Tokyo. Jane and Ben try to forget the scary experience, but they can't. Then Ben's shoulder starts to hurt all the time. When Ben looks at his photos, there are strange images of a girl. Is it the girl from the road?

[1] A *shutter* is part of a camera. When you take a photo, it opens and lets light into the camera.

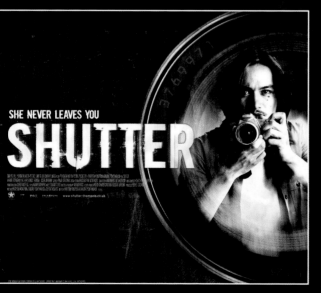

A The article is about two movies: an original and a remake. Answer the questions with a partner.

1. What is a remake?

2. What famous movie remakes do you know?

3. The name of both movies is *Shutter*. Look at the posters. What type of movie do you think it is?

B Work with a new partner. Complete the task.

Student A: Read about the original movie. Complete the sentences.

Student B: Read about the remake. Complete the sentences.

1. The two main characters are a man and a woman named _____ and _____.

2. The man and woman know each other. They are _____ and _____.

3. The man works as a _____.

4. They are _____ in the country late at night.

5. They have an accident. They hit _____.

6. They return home to _____.

7. Later the man has pain in his _____.

8. There are strange things in the man's _____.

C Take turns asking your partner questions about the information in **B**. How are the two movies different?

> 66 Who are the two main characters?
>
> Tun and Jane. Tun is a man, and Jane is a woman. 99

> 66 In the remake, the man's name is different . . .

D **Discuss findings.** Answer the questions with your partner.

1. What do you think happens next in the movie? Do you think it ends happily?

2. Do you want to see *Shutter* (the original or the remake)? Why or why not?

3. Some movies are classics and do not make good remakes. Name two movies that this is true for. Why do you think the originals are so good?

LISTENING

A Work with a partner. Discuss the questions.

  1. Where do you usually watch movie trailers?

  2. Do you always watch the trailer before you see a movie? Why or why not?

B Read the sentences. Then listen to two people talking about new movies and choose your answers. 🎧94

  1. The man **likes** / **dislikes** the *Fast Cars* movies because they're **exciting** / **original** / **violent**.

  2. The woman **likes** / **dislikes** the *Fast Cars* movies because they're **exciting** / **original** / **violent**.

  3. The man **likes** / **dislikes** Laura Swift because she's **boring** / **funny** / **talented**.

  4. Laura's new movie is a **comedy** / **drama** / **documentary**.

  5. The woman says the movie has a **funny** / **sad** / **surprising** ending.

C Listen again. Complete each sentence with one word. 🎧94

  1. *Fast Cars 4* is _____ out in a few days.

  2. It had the same _____ as the last one.

  3. Laura Swift's movie is about a big _____.

  4. They all come together for the _____.

  5. The movie opens _____.

D Think about movies you know. Make some notes about one with a surprise ending. Then tell a partner about it.

WORD BANK

A **movie trailer** is an ad for a new movie. It is usually around two minutes long and shows scenes from the movie.

A: When is that movie **coming out**?
B: It **opens** July 1st. I can't wait to see it!

In the past, people only saw movie trailers at the movie theater.

GRAMMAR

A   Read the Unit 12, Lesson B Grammar Reference in the appendix. Complete the exercises. Then do the exercises below.

-ED ADJECTIVES	*-ING* ADJECTIVES
I'm **bored**. I don't like this movie. I was **surprised** by the ending.	This movie is **boring**. Let's watch something else. The end of the movie was **surprising**.
Use *-ed* adjectives for people. *I'm bored* means "I feel bored."	Use *-ing* adjectives for people, things, or experiences. *This movie is boring* means, "This movie is making me feel bored."

B   Choose the correct answers.

1. Do your favorite movies always have **amazed** / **amazing** special effects?
2. Do you like to be **frightened** / **frightening** when you go to the movies?
3. Does the story have to be **interested** / **interesting** for a movie to be **entertained** / **entertaining**?
4. Are you **interested** / **interesting** in many different types of movies?
5. Do you like a **surprised** / **surprising** ending?
6. When you see a **depressed** / **depressing** movie, are you sad for a long time?
7. Are you easily **confused** / **confusing** by a difficult story?
8. Do you always enjoy going to the movies, or do you sometimes feel **bored** / **boring**?

C   Ask five classmates the questions in **B**. Write their names and **Y** if they answer *yes* and **N** for *no*.

Question	Student 1 _____	Student 2 _____	Student 3 _____	Student 4 _____	Student 5 _____
1					
2					
3					
4					
5					
6					
7					
8					

D   Write five more sentences about the information you collected in **C**. Tell the class.

1. Many students like to be frightened at the movies. Horror movies are very popular!
2. _____
3. _____
4. _____
5. _____
6. _____

ACTIVE ENGLISH Try it out!

A Think of a movie you like. Complete the information.

Name of movie: _____

1. What type of movie is it?
   _____

2. Who are the main characters?
   _____

3. Where does the story happen?
   _____

4. When does it take place?
   _____

5. What is the movie about?
   _____

6. What is your favorite scene?
   _____

B Ask a partner the questions in **A**. Guess the name of your partner's movie.

❝ | What type of movie is it?

It's a sci-fi movie. | ❞

C What do you think of your partner's movie? Use the sentences to explain.
- I also saw [name of movie], and I **liked / didn't like** it because . . .
- I didn't know about [name of movie], but now I'd like to see it because . . .
- I don't plan to see [name of movie] because . . .

❝ | I didn't know about . . . but now I'd like to
see it because it sounds interesting.

D **WRITING** Write about one of your favorite movies. Turn to the Writing appendix to see an example. Then complete the task. Use your notes from **A**.
1. Introduce the movie and tell the story.
2. Write about your favorite scene and how you feel when you watch the movie.

12B GOALS   Now I can . . .

Give an opinion of a movie _____	1. Yes, I can.
Review a movie _____	2. Mostly, yes.
	3. Not yet.

GLOBAL VOICES

A You are going to watch four people talk about their favorite movies. How many do you know? Match each movie title and type of movie.

1. *Twilight*   a. Fantasy / Adventure
2. *Harry Potter*   b. Romance / Drama
3. *Titanic*   c. Fantasy / Romance
4. *Legally Blond*   d. Romantic comedy

B Watch the video. Choose **T** for *true* or **F** for *false*.

1. Alexandra liked *Harry Potter* because it took her to a different world.   **T F**
2. Ai was surprised that the main character graduated from Harvard University.   **T F**
3. Francielen was happy with the ending in *Titanic*.   **T F**
4. Daniele thought the ending of *Twilight* was sad.   **T F**

C Watch the video again. Complete the sentences.

1. I know, it's an _____ movie.
2. I was _____ by the special effects they used.
3. The *Harry Potter* ending was _____.
4. I was so _____ and encouraged by her graduation speech.
5. They ended up as a family, and this is really _____.

D Think of your favorite movie. Read the questions and make notes.

1. What is the name of the movie? What kind of movie is it?
2. What surprised you about the movie?
3. What happened at the end of the movie?

E Tell a partner about your favorite movie. Use your notes from **D**.

The Harry Potter
movies were popular
all over the world.

REAL WORLD LINK WHAT DID YOU LEARN?

Students in Fujian, China celebrate after finishing a college entrance exam.

A Congratulations! You finished *World Link* 1. Complete the task. Make notes in your notebook.

Turn to . . .

1. the scope and sequence at the start of the book.

2. the grammar pages in each unit.

3. the Active English pages and look at the lesson goals.

Think about these questions:

What topics were you most interested in? Why?

Which grammar points were you good at? Which ones were difficult?

When did you check *Yes, I can*?
When did you check *Not yet*?

B A student is going to talk about her experience learning English. Read. Then listen and complete the sentences. 95

When she started class, she felt (1.) _____, but she was also (2.) _____ to start practicing English again.

When she first started, she couldn't use the (3.) _____ at all.

Now she **can / can't** do it because she (4.) _____ a lot in class and on her own. It's really (5.) _____ for her because she (6.) _____ about many more things.

For her, (7.) _____ is still difficult, especially when people (8.) _____.

Her advice:

- (9.) _____ in English.
- Don't try to (10.) _____ everything—just (11.) _____ on the main points.

She wants to keep learning, so she's (12.) _____ this summer. She's also going to work on improving her (13.) _____.

C Complete the questionnaire about your own experience learning English. Use your notes in **A** to help you.

COURSE QUESTIONNAIRE

At the start of the course

1. When you first started the course, how did you feel? Why did you feel this way?

   curious   excited   full of energy   nervous   relaxed   other: _____

   _____

What I learned

2. When you first started the course, what *couldn't* you do? List one or two things.

   _____

3. Can you do these things now? Why or why not?

   _____

4. Complete the sentence: For me, _____ is still difficult.

My advice

5. Think about your experience. Give some advice about learning English successfully.

   DO: _____

   DON'T: _____

Next steps

6. Are you taking another English class? How do you plan to keep learning?

   _____

D **You Choose** You are going to tell your classmates about your experience learning English. Choose an option. Use your information in **C** to explain.

Option 1: Write about your experience.

Option 2: Make a short video about your experience.

Option 3: Prepare an in-class presentation about your experience.

E Work in a small group. Learn about each classmate's experience. After each classmate is done, complete the task.

1. Think about your classmate's answer to Question 4 in **C**. Give your classmate some advice.

2. Compliment your classmate on successfully completing the class.

LANGUAGE SUMMARIES

UNIT 1: PEOPLE

LESSON A	LESSON B
Vocabulary	**Vocabulary**

LESSON A

Vocabulary

city
email address
first / last name
friends
hometown
job
languages
phone number

interested in (something)

subject

LESSON B

Vocabulary

be +
  young / **old**
  in your teens / **twenties**
  thin / **average weight** / **heavy**
  short / **average height** / **tall**

have +
  brown / **blue** / **green eyes**
  long / **short** / **straight** / **curly hair**
  black / **brown** / **blond** / **red hair**

  look like

good-looking
handsome
pretty
petite

a beard
a mustache

be +
  in great shape

have +
  a nice smile
  a friendly face

Speaking Strategy

Introducing Yourself
A: My name is Mariana.
B: Hi, I'm Danny. (It's) Nice to meet you.
A: (It's) Nice to meet you, too.

Asking Questions
A: What do you do?
B: I'm a music student.

When you are introducing yourself, *My name is . . .* and *I'm . . .* can both be used.

UNIT 2: BEHAVIOR

LESSON A

Vocabulary

laugh
look
run
shout
smile
start
stop
watch
wave
wear

throw

LESSON B

Vocabulary

afraid (of something)
angry
bored
excited
happy
nervous
relaxed
sad
tired
worried

miss

Calm down.
Good luck.
Hang in there.
I'm so excited!

Speaking Strategy

Greeting People and Asking How They Are

A: Hi, . . . How's it going?
B: Fine. / OK. / All right. / Pretty good. How are you (doing)?
A: I'm fine.

A: Hi, . . . How are you doing?
B: So-so.
A: Yeah? What's up?
B: I have a lot of homework.

UNIT 3: SHOPPING

LESSON A	LESSON B
Vocabulary **fresh** / **frozen** / **junk** food **apples, bananas, carrots, grapes** **beef, chicken, fish** **bread, soup** **butter, sugar** **cake, ice cream** **cereal, cheese, eggs, milk, yogurt** **chips, french fries** **coffee, juice, tea** **lettuce, salad, tomatoes** **noodles, rice, tofu** **a bottle of** orange juice / water **a box of** cereal **a bunch of** bananas / carrots / grapes **a can of** soda / soup **a carton of** eggs / ice cream **a head of** lettuce **a loaf of** bread **a piece of** cake	**Vocabulary** **buy** cash **go shopping** credit card **pay** refund **return** **sell** **spend** **try on**

Speaking Strategy
Talking About Things You Need

What do we have?	We have coffee and donuts.
What else do we need?	We still need plates and napkins. Nothing. We have everything.
Do we need anything else?	Yes, we (still) need cream and sugar. No, that's it. We have everything.

Use *still* for unfinished actions. It comes before the verb.

UNIT 4: VACATION

LESSON A		LESSON B	
Vocabulary		**Vocabulary**	
cloudy	clear	**buy a ticket**	flight
sunny	dry season	**go sightseeing**	passport
windy	rainy season	**pack a suitcase**	
raining		**take a trip**	
snowing		**take photos**	
chilly / cool			
cold			
comfortable			
freezing			
hot			
warm			
degrees			

Speaking Strategy

Giving Advice	**Accepting**	**Refusing**
You should take a jacket.	Good idea. / OK, I will.	(Thanks, but) I'll be OK.
I don't think you should wear shorts. You shouldn't wear shorts.	Yeah, you're right.	Don't worry. (I'll be OK.)

UNIT 5: HEROES

LESSON A	LESSON B
Vocabulary	**Vocabulary**
author photographer	**admire** kindness
educator	**caring**
explorer	**friendly** make someone's
pilot	**generous** day
presenter	**helpful**
researcher	**kind**
scientist	**selfish**
speaker	**strangers**
teacher	**together**
traveler	**warm**
writer	

Speaking Strategy

Agreeing and Disagreeing with an Opinion

I think *Hidden Figures* is a good movie.

Agreeing	**Disagreeing**
I think so, too. /	Really? I don't think so. /
I agree.	Sorry, but I disagree.
Follow-up Question	**Follow-up Question**
What do you like	Why do you say that?
about it?	

You can agree or disagree with a negative statement by saying *me neither*.

A: I don't like that movie.
B: Me neither.

UNIT 6: THE MIND

LESSON A	LESSON B
Vocabulary	**Vocabulary**
forget ↔ **remember**	**dream** energetic
easy / hard to ~	**fall asleep** ↔ **stay awake** energy
	go to bed sleep in
memory	**rest** stay up (late)
have a good / bad ~	**sleep** ↔ **wake up** take a nap
a happy / sad ~	a waste of time
recognize	

Speaking Strategy

Expressing Degrees of Certainty

Is your phone in your backpack?

Yes, it is. / No, it isn't.	(very certain)
I think so. / I don't think so	(less certain)
Maybe. I'm not sure.	(not very certain)
I don't know. / I have no idea.	(not certain at all)

UNIT 7: CITY LIFE

LESSON A	LESSON B
Vocabulary	**Vocabulary**
bookstore block	delay
department store corner	journey
grocery store (supermarket)	passenger
	pollute
bus station	polluted
gas station	pollution
police station	system
subway station	traffic
train station	transportation
hair salon	
nail salon	
health club (gym)	
nightclub	

Speaking Strategy

Asking for Directions	**Giving Directions**
Are you familiar with this neighborhood?	
Do you know this neighborhood?	
Is there a gas station near here?	Yes, there's one on First Avenue. / Yes, it's on First Avenue.
Where's the nearest gas station?	There's one on First Avenue. / It's on First Avenue.
How do I get there from here?	Go straight. / Turn right. / Turn left.
	It's on the right / left.
	It's on the corner.

UNIT 8: ALL ABOUT YOU

LESSON A	LESSON B
Vocabulary	**Vocabulary**
go + *play +*	ambitious kind of / a little
biking baseball	careful very / really
hiking basketball	careless
rock climbing cards	easy-going
rollerblading field hockey	messy
running golf	neat
skateboarding pool	shy
skiing soccer	talkative
surfing tennis	
swimming video games	

Speaking Strategy

Inviting Others to Do Something	**Saying *Yes***	**Saying *No***
Do you want to come?	(Sure,) Sounds good.	(Thanks, but) I can't.
Would you like to come?	(Sure,) I'd love to.	I'd love to, but . . .

Would you like to . . . is a little more formal than *Do you want to.*

UNIT 9: CHANGE

LESSON A	LESSON B
Vocabulary	**Vocabulary**

habit   in the habit of
  a good / bad ~ (doing something)
  a healthy / unhealthy ~
  break a bad ~
  build a good ~
  have a ~ of doing
    something
	plastic
	  ~bag
	  ~bottle
	  ~cup
	  ~straw

make a change	**goal** **million(s)** **recycle** **reuse**
annoying **bother** **fail**	**trash** **It takes** (+ period of time)

Speaking Strategy

Making Requests	**Positive Response**	**Negative Response**
Can / Could I borrow your ladder? Can / Could you bring it tomorrow?	Sure. No problem. / Of course. / Certainly.	I'm sorry, but . . .

UNIT 10: HEALTH

LESSON A	LESSON B
Vocabulary	**Vocabulary**
arm(s) muscle	**stress** tense
back	**stressed**
chest fever	**stressful**
foot / feet headache	
hand(s) stomachache	**energy**
head	**full of ~**
ear(s)	**low on ~**
eye(s)	
face	**anxiety**
nose	**focus**
mouth	**last**
leg(s)	
neck	
shoulder(s)	
stomach	
long ↔ short (arms / legs)	
big / large ↔ little / small (eyes / nose)	

Speaking Strategy	
Talking about Health Problems	
What's wrong?	I don't feel well.
What's the matter?	I'm sick. / I'm tired.
	I have a fever.
	My arm hurts.
(I'm) Sorry to hear that.	

UNIT 11: ACHIEVEMENT

LESSON A	LESSON B
Vocabulary	**Vocabulary**
ability genius	**brave**
good at (something)	**curious**
practice	**dangerous**
special	**difficult**
succeed	**safe**
success	**take a chance**
successful	
talent	
talented	

Speaking Strategy	
Complimenting	**Reply**
Great / Good job!	Thanks.
. . . is amazing / really good.	Thank you.
You're a great . . .	That's nice of you to say.
I like . . . a lot.	
You can . . . really well.	

UNIT 12: AT THE MOVIES

LESSON A		LESSON B	
Vocabulary		**Vocabulary**	
action movie	animated movie	**boring**	come out
classic movie	biopic	**entertaining**	open
documentary	blockbuster	**exciting**	
drama	sequel	**funny**	
horror movie		**original**	
romantic comedy		**scary**	
science fiction (sci-fi)		**surprising**	
		violent	
		character	

Speaking Strategy

Starting a Phone Call	**Ending a Phone Call**	**Asking Someone to Repeat**
Hello?	See you (later / soon). / Bye.	(Sorry,) I didn't hear you. Can you repeat that?
Hi. It's . . .		(Sorry,) I didn't catch that. Can you say that again?

1 PEOPLE

LESSON A

REVIEW OF THE SIMPLE PRESENT							
Affirmative Statements			**Negative Statements**				
I / You / We / They	**speak**	English.	I / You / We / They	*don't*	**speak**	English.
He / She / It	**speaks**		He / She / It	*doesn't*		

Yes / No Questions with *Be*					**Short Answers**	
Is	she	a	student?	Yes, she **is**.	No, *she's* **not**.* / No, *she* **isn't**.
Are	you			Yes, I **am**.	No, *I'm* **not**.
	they		students?	Yes, they **are**.	No, *they're* **not**.* / No, *they* **aren't**.
*In spoken English, this negative form is more common.						

Yes / No Questions with Other Verbs				**Answers**	
Do	you	**speak**	English?	Yes, I **do**.	No, I *don't*.
Does	she			Yes, she **does**.	No, *she* **doesn't**.

Wh- Questions				**Answers**
Where	**do**	you	**live**?	I **live** in Buenos Aires.
	does	he		He still **lives** in his hometown.
What	**do**	you	**do**?	I'm a student.
	does	she		She's a doctor.

A Complete the questions and answers. Then match each question to an appropriate answer.

1. _____ you live alone?
2. _____ _____ you do for fun?
3. _____ you a good student?
4. _____ _____ you live with?
5. _____ you a teacher?
6. _____ is your part-time job?

a. No, _____ _____. I'm a student.
b. My mother and father.
c. Yes, _____ _____. I get good grades.
d. I'm in a band.
e. I'm an office clerk.
f. No, I _____. I live with my family.

B Work with a partner. Ask and answer the questions in **A**.

DESCRIBING APPEARANCE

Subject	Be / Have	Adjective	Noun
He	is	short / tall.	
		average	height / weight.
		young / in his teens.	
	has	blue / brown / green	eyes.
		long / straight / black	hair.

Use *be* to describe a person's height, weight, and age.

Use *have* to describe a person's eyes and hair.*

*The exceptions: *He is bald.* (He has no hair on his head.)
He is clean-shaven. (He has no hair on his face.)

When using two or more adjectives, the words usually follow this pattern: length, style, color.

*He has **short, curly, red** hair.*   *She has **big blue** eyes.*

A Complete the sentences with the correct form of *be* or *have*.

1. Tanya's dad _____ tall.

2. Rita and her brother _____ curly hair.

3. My cousin _____ in her teens. She _____ young.

4. I _____ green eyes.

5. Max and Charlie are friends. Max _____ a beard and mustache. Charlie _____ clean-shaven. They both _____ blond hair.

6. Damon _____ average weight.

B Look at the photo and complete the sentences about Lupita Nyong'o.

Her name (1.) _____ Lupita Nyong'o.

She (2.) _____ an actor.

Her hometown (3.) _____ Nairobi, Kenya.

She (4.) _____ black hair.

She (5.) _____ brown eyes.

She's young. She (6.) _____ in her thirties.

She (7.) _____ pretty.

C Tell a partner about Lupita Nyong'o.

Lupita Nyong'o is a famous actor.

LESSON A

THE PRESENT CONTINUOUS: AFFIRMATIVE AND NEGATIVE STATEMENTS			
❶ I'm / You're / She's / They're	(not)	**studying**	for a big test.
❷ I'm / You're / She's / They're		**working**	hard these days.

The present continuous: subject + *am / is / are* + verb + *-ing*

I am → I'm   You are → You're   She is → She's   They are → They're

Use the present continuous to talk about . . .

   ❶ actions happening right now.

   ❷ actions happening for a period of time in the present (*these days*, *this week*).

study → studying   *smile → smiling*   *stop → stopping*

YES / NO AND WH- QUESTIONS				
Question Word	***Be***		**Verb + *-ing***	**Answers**
	Are	you		Yes, I am. / No, I'm not.
	Is	she	**studying?**	Yes, she is. / No, she's not.
	Are	they		Yes, they are. / No, they're not.
What	**are**	you		(I'm studying) English.
Where	**is**	she	**studying?**	(She's studying) at school.
Why	**are**	they		(They're studying) Because they have a test.

A   Make sentences with the present continuous. Use contractions when possible.

1. _____I'm wearing_____ (I, wear) my glasses today.
   _____I'm not wearing_____ (I, not, wear) my contact lenses.
2. _Tomas is watching_ (Tomas, watch) TV with his friends.
3. _Erika and Martin are running_ (Erika and Martin, run) in the Color Run race, and
   They're winning (they, win).
4. _We are using_ (we, use) this book in our English class this term.
5. _She isn't going_ (she, not, go) to school anymore.
   She is living (she, live) in the UK these days.

B Complete each conversation. Where can you use short answers?

1. A: _Are you doing_ _____ (you, do) your homework?
   B: No, _I don't a am not_ _____.
   A: _What are you doing_ _____ (do)?
   B: _I am watching_ _____ (watch) a video.

2. A: _Are Is your brother living_ _____ (your brother, live) in the US these days?
   B: No, _he isn't_ _____.
   A: _Where are you living_ _____ (live)?
   B: _I am living and working_ _____ (live and work) in Canada.

3. A: _Are you and your sister running_ _____ (you and your sister, run) every day?
   B: Yes, _They're not_ _____.
   A: _Are you running_ _____ (run) every day?
   B: _Yes, I am_ _running_ (run) every day because _I am preparing_ (prepare) for a race.

4. A: _Are Oscar and Fiona shouting_ _____ (Oscar and Fiona, shout)?
   B: Yes, _They're_ _____.
   A: _Why are you shouting_ _____ (shout)?
   B: _Because I'm watching a_ _____ (watch) a soccer game.
       They're

C Read the questions. Circle the correct answers.

1. Which conversations talk about something happening right now?

   Conversation 1   Conversation 2   Conversation 3   (Conversation 4)

2. Which conversations talk about something happening these days?

   Conversation 1   (Conversation 2)   Conversation 3   Conversation 4

SUBJECT PRONOUNS			OBJECT PRONOUNS		
Subject	Verb	Object	Subject	Verb	Object
I	don't like	spiders.	Spiders	scare	me.
You					you.
He / She	doesn't like				him / her.
We	don't like				us.
They					them.
It	is	a big dog.	I'm afraid of		it.

In a sentence, an object pronoun can replace a noun.
*I don't like **spiders**. ↔ I don't like **them**.*

An object pronoun comes after a <u>verb</u> or a <u>preposition</u>.
*Spiders <u>scare</u> **me**.*
*I'm afraid <u>of</u> **them**.*

A Read the sentences. Underline the subject. Circle the object.

1. Carla is talking to her brother.
2. Tomas is smiling at Jane.
3. Carlos and I are worried about the test.
4. Some people are afraid of dogs.
5. Are you and Haru going to the game now?
6. Rick and I can meet you and Mike at 3:00.
7. The dog is sitting with Nick and me on the sofa.
8. Maya is texing David.

B Rewrite the sentences in **A**. Use the correct subject and object pronouns.

1. *She is / She's talking to him.* _____
2. _____
3. _____
4. _____
5. _____
6. _____
7. _____
8. _____

SHOPPING

LESSON A

COUNT NOUNS		NONCOUNT NOUNS			
Singular	**Plural**				English divides nouns into things we can count (count nouns) and things we can't (noncount nouns). Count nouns have a plural form (apple → apples). Noncount nouns don't (beef → ~~beefs~~).
apple carrot tomato	apples carrots tomatoes	beef bread cereal	cheese garlic meat	oil rice soda	

SINGULAR AND PLURAL COUNT NOUNS; NONCOUNT NOUNS					
	Article	**Noun**	**Verb**		
Singular Count Nouns	A	banana	is	a good snack.	Use *a / an* or *the* before the noun.
	The	banana	is	in the bowl.	Use a singular form of the verb.
Plural Count Nouns	—	Bananas	are	good for you.	Use *the* before the noun.
	The	bananas	are	on the table.	Use a plural form of the verb.
Noncount Nouns	—	Bread	is	inexpensive.	Use *the* before the noun.
	The	bread	is	in the bag.	Use a singular form of the verb.

TALKING ABOUT AMOUNTS							
General Amount			**Specific Amount**				
Please buy	**some**	bread.	Please buy	a	**loaf**	of	bread.
		lettuce.			**head**		lettuce.
		eggs.			**carton**		eggs.
		grapes.			**bunch**		grapes.
a bottle of water a can of soup / soda		a glass of juice / water a piece of cake / chocolate			a cup of coffee / soup a slice of bread / pie		

A Read the recipe for beef stir fry. Circle the count nouns. Underline the noncount nouns.

Pour some (1.) **oil** into (2.) a **pan** and heat it up. Add some (3.) **garlic**, (4.) **mushrooms**, and (5.) **carrots** into the pan and cook them. Remove the garlic and (6.) the **vegetables** from the pan. Next, cook (7.) the **beef**. Put (8.) the **meat** and (9.) **vegetables** together and cover with (10.) **soy sauce**. Serve over (11.) **rice** on (12.) a **dinner plate**.

B Write the missing words.

1. I'm thirsty. May I have a ____drink____ of water, please?

2. He always has a _____ of bread and a _____ of soup for lunch.

3. Please bring two ____drink____ of water on the hike.

4. I enjoy a ____cup____ of tea every morning.

5. It's my mother's birthday. I have a _____ of flowers for her.

QUANTIFIERS WITH AFFIRMATIVE AND NEGATIVE STATEMENTS			
Plural Count Nouns	I have	a lot of / many some	jackets.
	I don't have	a lot of / many any	
Noncount Nouns	I have	a lot of / — some	cash.
	I don't have	a lot of / much any	

Large Amount
↑ a lot of / many some not a lot of / not much / not many ↓
Small Amount

Use quantifiers to talk about amounts.

A lot of / many refer to large amounts. We don't use *much* in the affirmative.

~~I have much jackets.~~

Not a lot of / not much / not many refer to small amounts.

I don't have any cash = I have no cash.

	YES / NO QUESTIONS WITH ANY		SHORT ANSWERS	
Plural Count Nouns	Do you have **any**	jackets?	Yes, I do.	No, I don't.
Noncount Nouns		cash?		

Use *any* in *Yes / No* questions to ask about general amounts.
Answer these questions with a short answer.

A Circle the best answer in each sentence.

1. Juan has $1,000,000. He has **much** / **a lot of** ✓ cash.

2. Barry only has $2. He doesn't have **any** / **much** cash.

3. This store only sells clothes. You can't buy **any** ✓ / **many** shoes here.

4. Rita has **a lot of** ✓ / **many** beautiful jewelry.

5. There aren't **much** / **many** department stores in this city. There are only two.

6. Leo has three friends. He has **many** / **some** friends.

B Complete each sentence with a quantifier. Then practice the exchanges with a partner.

1. **A:** Do you have ____any____ questions about the homework?

   B: No, I don't have ____any____. I understand everything.

2. **A:** Are there ____many____ girls in this class?

   B: Yes, there are ____many____—three or four, I think.

3. **A:** Do you have _____ cash?

   B: Yes, I do. But I don't have _____. I only have five dollars.

4. **A:** Is there _____ room in the closet for my suitcase?

   B: Yes, the closet is empty. There's _____ room.

VACATION

LESSON A

CONNECTING IDEAS WITH *BUT*, *OR*, AND *SO*	
It's sunny **but** cool today. It's a nice day **but** a little chilly. It's warm in the afternoon, **but** it's cold at night.	Use *but* to show a contrast (a difference). *But* joins words, phrases, and clauses.
Let's visit Montreal in June **or** July. We can stay with my family **or** with friends. We can walk, **or** we can ride our bikes.	Use *or* to give choices. *Or* joins words, phrases, and clauses.
It's chilly, **so** you should take a jacket.	Use *so* to introduce a result. *So* joins clauses.
Use a comma when *but*, *or*, and *so* join two clauses (phrases with a noun and a verb).	

A Complete the sentences with *but*, *or*, or *so*.

1. William can't speak French, _____ Marion can.

2. Does our vacation start this week _____ next week?

3. It's warm outside, _____ I don't think you need a jacket.

4. When does our plane leave: at 7:00 _____ 7:30?

5. Tokyo is an exciting city, _____ it's very expensive to live there.

6. It's 32 degrees out, _____ I'm wearing a T-shirt.

7. It's snowing outside, _____ Mario is wearing shorts.

8. Please call _____ text me later.

B Combine the two sentences using *but*, *or*, or *so*.

1. Kaz likes to travel. His girlfriend doesn't like to travel.

   Kaz likes to travel, but his girlfriend doesn't (like to travel).

2. We can go to Martin's party. We can see a movie.

   _____

3. John is sick. He's not coming to class today.

   _____

4. It's a beautiful day. We're having class outside.

   _____

5. I'm wearing my glasses. I can't see the whiteboard.

   _____

6. Rosa wants to study at an American university. She's taking the TOEFL exam.

   _____

LESSON B

POSSESSIVE ADJECTIVES		
I have a passport.	**My** passport is green.	We use possessive adjectives for ownership and relationships.
You have a passport.	**Your** passport is green.	*His passport is green.*
She has a passport	**Her** passport is green.	*That woman is **her** mother.*
He has a passport.	**His** passport is green.	
We have tickets.	**Our** tickets are free.	Possessive adjectives go before nouns.
They have tickets.	**Their** tickets are free.	

WHOSE	POSSESSIVE PRONOUNS		
Whose passport is this?	It's **mine**.	We use possessive pronouns for ownership. *That ticket is **mine**.*	**ℹ️ *Belong to*** You can also use *belong* to to talk about ownership: *It's mine. = It belongs to me.*
	It's **yours**.		
	It's **hers**.	They come after the verb *be*.	
	It's **his**.		
Whose tickets are these?	They're **ours**.	Use *whose* to ask about ownership.	
	They're **theirs**.		

A Write the correct possessive pronouns for the underlined words.

1. **A:** That's not her suitcase.

   B: No, <u>her suitcase</u> is over there. *hers*

2. **A:** Can I use your cell phone? <u>My cell phone</u> isn't working.

   B: Sorry, but I forgot my cell phone. Use <u>Jon's phone</u>.

3. **A:** Is your class fun?

   B: Yes, but <u>Aya and Leo's class</u> is more interesting.

4. **A:** Is your hometown hot in the summer? <u>My hometown</u> is.

   B: <u>Our hometown</u> is, too.

5. **A:** Your birthday is in May.

   B: That's right, and <u>your birthday</u> is in March.

B Complete the conversation. Then practice it with a partner.

Jim: Well, I have (1.) _____ *my* _____ suitcase. Where's (2.) _____?

Ben: Um . . . let's see . . . oh, here's (3.) _____ suitcase. No, wait . . . this one isn't (4.) _____.

Jim: (5.) _____ is it?

Ben: It says Mr. Simon Konig. It belongs to (6.) _____.

Jim: Hey, I think that man has (7.) _____ suitcase. See? He probably thinks it's (8.) _____.

Ben: I'll ask him. Excuse me, does this suitcase belong to (9.) _____?

Simon: Oh, no. Do I have (10.) _____ suitcase? Sorry about that!

5 HEROES

LESSON A

THE SIMPLE PAST WITH *BE*							
AFFIRMATIVE AND NEGATIVE STATEMENTS			**YES / NO QUESTIONS**			**ANSWERS**	
Subject	*Was / Were*		*Was / Were*	Subject			
I	**was** / wasn't	a scientist.	**Were**	you	a scientist?	Yes, I **was**. / No, I **wasn't**.	
You	**were** / weren't			they	scientists?	Yes, they **were**. / No, they **weren't**.	
He / She	**was** / wasn't		**Was**	she	a scientist?	Yes, she **was**. / No, she **wasn't**.	
We / You / They	**were** / weren't	scientists.					

WH- QUESTIONS				ANSWERS
Wh- Word	*Was / Were*	Subject		
Where	**were**	you	yesterday?	At home.
When	**was**	he	in Antarctica?	A year ago.
Who	**was**	your teacher	last semester?	Ms. Hunter.
Use time expressions with the simple past: *yesterday*, *two days ago*, *last semester*.				

A Complete the conversation with a partner. Use the correct form of the verb *be* in the simple past.

Tim: Hi, Kelly. It's Tim. I called you yesterday, but you (1.) _____ (not) home.

Kelly: I (2.) _____ at the library. I'm writing a paper about Pierre and Marie Curie.

Tim: They (3.) _____ scientists from France, right?

Kelly: Right. Well, actually Pierre (4.) _____ French, but his wife (5.) _____ (not) born in France. She (6.) _____ from Poland. She (7.) _____ also the first person to win a Nobel Prize twice.

B Complete the questions. Then match them with the correct answers.

1. _____ Kelly at home?
2. _____ _____ Kelly?
3. _____ the Curies scientists?
4. _____ Marie Curie born in Poland?
5. _____ _____ Marie Curie born?
6. _____ Pierre Curie the first person to win two Nobel Prizes?
7. _____ _____ Pierre Curie from?
8. _____ _____ the Curies?

a. Yes, they were.
b. No, she wasn't.
c. No, he wasn't.
d. They were scientists.
e. Yes, she was.
f. France.
g. At the library.
h. Poland.

LESSON B

THE SIMPLE PAST: AFFIRMATIVE AND NEGATIVE STATEMENTS		
I / You / He / She / We / They	**visited**	Tokyo.
	didn't visit	
I / You / He / She / We / They	**started**	a company.
	didn't start	

In the simple past, the verb form is the same for all persons.
In affirmative statements, add -*ed* or -*d*. See the spelling rules.
In negative statements, use *didn't (did not)* + the base form of the verb.

THE SIMPLE PAST OF REGULAR VERBS: SPELLING RULES	
mov**e** → mov**ed**	If the verb ends in *e*, add -*d*.
star**t** → start**ed**	If the verb ends with a consonant, add -*ed*.
stu**dy** → stud**ied**	If the verb ends with a consonant + *y*, change the *y* to *i* and add -*ed*.
pl**ay** → play**ed**	If the verb ends with a vowel + *y*, add -*ed*.
sto**p** → stop**ped**	With one-syllable verbs that end with a consonant–vowel–consonant, double the last letter and add -*ed*.

A Write the simple past form of the verbs.

1. like _____
2. enjoy _____
3. want _____
4. try _____
5. work _____

6. change _____
7. plan _____
8. stay _____
9. carry _____
10. use _____

B Read about the Wall of Kindness. Complete the sentences with the simple past form of the verbs in the box.

have	~~learn~~	pick up	place	start	stay	stop	study

1. In school, we _____ *learned* _____ about different acts of kindness around the world.
2. We _____ the Wall of Kindness in Iran.
3. It _____ in the city of Mashad.
4. Some people in the city _____ (not) winter clothing or food.
5. As a gift, neighbors _____ clothing and food on a wall.
6. There was a sign that said, "Leave what you don't need. Take what you do." People _____ at the wall to look.
7. They _____ free clothing.
8. This tradition _____ (not) only in Iran. Other countries do it now, too!

THE MIND

LESSON A

THE SIMPLE PAST: AFFIRMATIVE AND NEGATIVE STATEMENTS (IRREGULAR VERBS)			
Subject	***Did + Not***	**Verb**	
I / You / He / She / We / They		**found**	the tickets.
	didn't	**find**	
In affirmative statements, do not add *-ed* to form irregular simple past verbs. See the chart for the simple past forms of many common irregular verbs.			
In negative statements, use *did not* or *didn't* + the base form of the verb.			

PRESENT	PAST	PRESENT	PAST	PRESENT	PAST	PRESENT	PAST	PRESENT	PAST
begin	began	fall	fell	have	had	put	put	speak	spoke
bring	brought	feel	felt	hear	heard	read	read*	take	took
buy	bought	find	found	know	knew	run	ran	teach	taught
come	came	forget	forgot	leave	left	say	said	tell	told
do	did	get	got	make	made	see	saw	think	thought
drink	drank	give	gave	meet	met	sing	sang	wear	wore
eat	ate	go	went	pay	paid	sleep	slept	write	wrote

There is a vowel shift in the simple past pronunciation of read. The vowel goes from /iː/ to /ɛ/.

A Complete the story with the simple past forms of the verbs in parentheses. Most of the verbs are irregular. Which ones are regular?

There (1.) _____ (be) a fire one day when I (2.) _____ (be) at school. It (3.) _____ (begin) around lunchtime. Soon, we all (4.) _____ (smell) smoke. Someone (5.) _____ (say) in a loud voice, "Fire!" Then we (6.) _____ (hear) the fire alarm. As we (7.) _____ (walk) down the hallway, I (8.) _____ (feel) the heat from the fire. We (9.) _____ (not say) anything—everyone was very quiet.

The fire truck (10.) _____ (come) quickly. The firefighters (11.) _____ (run) into the building and (12.) _____ (stop) the fire. After 30 minutes, we (13.) _____ (go) back into our school. Luckily, there (14.) _____ (not be) much damage. I will never forget that day.

B Take turns reading the story in **A** with a partner. Then explain the story in your own words. Can you tell the story with your book closed?

LESSON B

THE SIMPLE PAST: *YES / NO* QUESTIONS				
Did	Subject	Verb		Short Answers
Did	you	**rest** **wake up**	last night?	Yes, I did. / No, I didn't.
	he / she			Yes, he did. / No, he didn't.
	they			Yes, they did. / No, they didn't.

To ask a simple past *Yes / No* question, use *did* + subject + base form of the verb.
Short answers are the same for both regular and irregular verbs.

THE SIMPLE PAST: *WH-* QUESTIONS				
Wh- Word	*Did*	Subject	Verb	Answers
When	**did**	you he / she / it they	**study**?	(I / She / They studied) last night.
			wake up?	(I / She / They woke up) at 7:00.
What			**happened**?	I woke up late this morning.

A Circle the mistake in each exchange and correct it.

1. **A:** Did Mario stayed awake late last night?
   B: Yes, he did.

2. **A:** Did you forget your keys?
   B: No, I didn't forgot them.

3. **A:** Where did Julie went on her vacation?
   B: She went to Mexico.

4. **A:** What did happen to Yu and Amy?
   B: They slept late and missed the bus.

B Complete the exchanges with a simple past *Yes / No*, or *Wh-* question, or a short answer.

1. **A:** _____ last night?
   B: I went to bed at 10:00.

2. **A:** _____ well?
   B: No, I didn't sleep well. I had nightmares.

3. **A:** _____ before bed?
   B: No, _____. I never drink coffee before bed.

4. **A:** Did you eat before bed?
   B: Yes, _____.

5. **A:** _____ last night?
   B: I ate a piece of cake. Maybe that caused the bad dreams.

6. **A:** _____ about?
   B: I dreamed about zombies.

C Practice the exchanges in **B** with a partner.

CITY LIFE

LESSON A

PREPOSITIONS OF PLACE: *AT, ON, AND IN*	
A: Where are you? **B:** I'm **at** school. I'm **on** the second floor, **in** my classroom.	• Use *at* + building: *at the mall, at home* • Use *on* + floor: *on the top floor* • Use *in* + room: *in my office, in the kitchen*
A: Where is the gas station? **B:** It's **at** 30 First Avenue. / It's **on** First Avenue.	• Use *at* + address: *at 100 Smith Street* • Use *on* + street: *on Smith Street*

A Complete each sentence (1–4) with *at, on,* or *in.* Then read the sentences (a–b). Check (✓) the sentences that are true or write *U* if the information is unknown.

1. Maria is _____ home right now.

    a. _____ She's in her bedroom.

    b. _____ She's not at school.

2. The coffee shop is _____ 200 Sky Street.

    a. _____ It's on Sky Street.

    b. _____ It's on the corner.

3. It's _____ the middle of the block.

    a. _____ It's not on the corner.

    b. _____ It's a long block.

4. Our classroom is _____ the first floor.

    a. _____ It's in a big building.

    b. _____ You don't need to take the elevator.

B Complete the conversation with *at* or *on.* Then practice it with a partner.

A: Where are you?

B: I'm still (1.) _____ work!

A: Really? The movie starts in 25 minutes!

B: I know! Where is the theater again?

A: It's (2.) _____ Oak Street. Let's see . . . it's (3.) _____ 200 Oak Street, to be exact. The theater is (4.) _____ the third floor.

B: OK. Got it. I'm catching a taxi now. See you soon!

C Circle the correct words and complete the sentences with information about yourself.

1. I'm **at / on / in** school every day from _____ to _____.

2. My classroom is **at / on / in** the _____ floor.

3. There are a lot of _____ **at / on / in** my classroom.

4. My school is **at / on / in** a _____ street.

LESSON B

QUESTIONS AND ANSWERS WITH *HOW MANY* (PLURAL COUNT NOUNS)	
How many cars are there? 　　There are **a lot** / **many**. 　　There are **some** / **a few**. 　　*There aren't* **many**. 　　*There aren't* **any**.	**How many** cars are there? 　　**A lot.** / **Many.** 　　**Some.** / **A few.** 　　Not many. 　　None.
QUESTIONS AND ANSWERS WITH *HOW MUCH* (NONCOUNT NOUNS)	
How much pollution is there? 　　There is **a lot**. 　　There is **some** / **a little**. 　　*There isn't* **much**. 　　*There isn't* **any**.	**How much** pollution is there? 　　**A lot.** 　　**Some.** / **A little.** 　　Not much. 　　None.

How many is used to ask about plural count nouns.
How much is used to ask about noncount nouns.

It's common to answer a *how many* / *how much* question with a short answer.
　　A: *How many parks are there in your city?*
　　B: *A few.* (a few = a very small number)

A　Circle the correct answers.

1. There isn't **many** / **any** traffic on the road at the moment.

2. Yesterday, there was a lot of pollution, but today, there's only **a little** / **a few**.

3. How **many** / **much** people live in your neighborhood?

4. **A:** How **many** / **much** rain does this city get in the winter?

　　B: It gets **a lot** / **much**.

B　Write the missing words to complete the sentences.

1. **A:** How _____ bookstores are there in your city?

　　B: Not _____. Most people buy books online now.

2. **A:** How _____ traffic is there at 8:30 in the morning?

　　B: There's _____. You can be stuck in traffic for an hour or more.

3. **A:** How _____ friends do you have?

　　B: Only _____. I just moved here. I only know two or three people.

4. **A:** How _____ homework do we have tonight?

　　B: _____. The teacher didn't give us any.

5. **A:** Do you have _____ free time on the weekend?

　　B: I have _____—about an hour or two.

6. **A:** How _____ Thai restaurants are there in your city?

　　B: There aren't _____. We don't even have one.

C　Now ask and answer the questions in **B** with a partner. Use your own answers.

8 ALL ABOUT YOU

LESSON A

VERB + INFINITIVE / VERB + NOUN			
Subject	**Verb**	**Infinitive**	
I	**need**	to study	for a test.
She	**wants**	to meet	her friends later.
They	**like**	to go	biking together.
Subject	**Verb**	**Noun**	
I	**need**	help	with my homework.
She	**wants**	a new bike.	
They	**like**	biking*	together.
These verbs can be followed by a noun or an infinitive (to + verb): *forget, hate, learn, like, love, need, decide, plan, prepare, want*.			

*An -ing *word can be a noun.*

A Read the sentences. Write *correct* if the sentence is correct. Rewrite the sentence if it is incorrect.

1. Hector <u>loves to playing</u> soccer with friends.

   _____

2. After class, we <u>plan to go swimming</u> at the beach.

   _____

3. Gina <u>wants come</u> with us, but she <u>forgot to her bathing suit</u> at home.

   _____

4. I'm <u>learning to ski</u>. Do you <u>like ski</u>?

   _____

B For each picture, make a sentence about Jenna or the other people. Use the verbs.

_____   _____   _____

_____   _____   _____

_____   _____   _____

C Are any of the things about Jenna true for you? Make sentences about yourself in your notebook.

LESSON B

QUESTIONS AND ANSWERS WITH *HOW OFTEN*		
How often do you clean your room?		
(I clean it)	**every** day / week / month.	
	once / **twice** / **three times** / **several times** a week / month.	
	all the time / **once in a while**.	

How often asks about the frequency of an event.

Frequency expressions usually come at the end of a sentence.
*I clean my room **once a week**.*

Hardly ever and *never* come before a verb.
*I **hardly ever** / **never** <u>clean</u> my room.*

You can answer a *How often* question with the frequency expression only.
How often do you clean your room? **Once a week**.

Some expressions give a specific answer.
*I clean my room **every day** / **once a week**.*

All the time and *once in a while* are less specific.*
*I clean my room **once in a while**.*

*all the time = always   *once in a while = sometimes

A Find the mistake in each exchange and correct it. Then practice each exchange with a partner.

1. **A:** How often you play tennis?
   B: Every Sunday.

2. **A:** How often do you have English class?
   B: Once a week, on Monday and Friday.

3. **A:** Is the bus usually on time?
   B: No, it's all the time late.

4. **A:** How often does Maria see her brother?
   B: Hardly ever she sees him. He works in the UK.

B Look at Ricardo's weekly schedule. Answer the questions with a word or phrase in **bold** from the chart.

Monday	Tuesday	Wednesday	Thursday	Friday	Saturday	Sunday
Class: 9–12 Work: 1–4	Work: 10–2	Class: 9–12 Work: 1–4	Work: 10–2	Class: 9–12 Work: 1–4	Study group: 10–12 Work: 1–4	Work: 3–6

1. How often does Ricardo have class?   _____three times_____ a week

2. How often does Ricardo work?   _____ day

3. How often does Ricardo work from 10 to 2?   _____ a week

4. How often does Ricardo work from 1 to 4?   _____ a week

5. How often does Ricardo meet with his study group?   _____

9 CHANGE

LESSON A

		LIKE	INFINITIVE OR GERUND	
	I	**like**	**to organize** / **organizing**	things.
Do	you	**like**	**to organize** / **organizing**	things?

The infinitive (*to* + verb) or the gerund (*-ing* form) is used after *like*.

Use *like* to talk about things you enjoy doing in general.
  Most people don't like cleaning, but I like to organize things.

Use short answers with the question form.
  Do you like . . . ?   *Yes, I do. / No, I don't.*

WOULD			*LIKE*	INFINITIVE	
I	**would**		**like**	**to organize**	my room.
	Would	you	**like**	**to organize**	your room?

The infinitive (*to* + verb) is used after *would like*. In spoken English, we use the contracted form of *would* with a pronoun.
  I'd like to organize my room.

Use *would like* to talk about specific things you want to do in the future.
  My room is a mess. I'd like to organize it.

Use short answers with the question form.
  Would you like . . . ?   *Yes, I would. / No, I wouldn't.*

A Complete the chart with the correct forms.

	I would
you'd	
	he would
she'd	
	we would
they'd	

B Use the words in the box to complete the conversations. Then practice them with a partner.

I like	do you like	I'd like
I don't like	do you like	I'd like
you'd like	would you like	I'd like

A: This menu looks interesting. (1.) _____ to try something new, but I can't decide.

B: Well, what kind of food (2.) _____?

A: Let's see . . . (3.) _____ anything too strange, but (4.) _____ spicy food.

B: Then I think (5.) _____ the red curry. It's really spicy . . . and very delicious!

A: It sounds good. I think (6.) _____ that.

A: What changes (7.) _____ to make in the new year?

B: Well, for one, (8.) _____ to lose some weight. I'm out of shape.

A: I see. And, (9.) _____ to exercise?

B: Yes, I do.

A: Come with me to the gym tomorrow, then. We can work out together.

THE FUTURE WITH *BE GOING TO*					
Subject	***Be***	***(Not)***	***Going To***	**Base Form**	
I	**am**	*not*	**going to**	buy	a reusable water bottle.
You	**are**				
He / She	**is**				
We / They	**are**				

Use *be going to* + the base form of a verb to talk about definite future plans. When the subject is a pronoun, use a contraction.

    I'm going to buy a reusable water bottle.

    I'm not going to use plastic bags.

We often use a future time expression with *be going to*.

    I'm going to buy a new water bottle <u>tomorrow</u> / <u>this weekend</u> / <u>next week</u> / <u>after class</u>.

    Kenya is going to ban all plastic bags <u>next year</u> / <u>in January</u>.

You can also use *be going to* to make predictions.

    The plastic ban is going to help Kenya.

YES / NO QUESTIONS					SHORT ANSWERS	
Is	she	**going to**	buy	a new bottle?	Yes, she is.	No, she's not. / No, she isn't.
Are	you				Yes, I am.	No, I'm not.
	they				Yes, they are.	No, they're not. / No, they aren't.

WH- QUESTIONS						ANSWERS
What				buy?		(I'm going to buy) a new water bottle.
When	**are**	you	**going to**	buy	it?	(I'm going to buy it) tomorrow.
Why						(I'm going to buy it) because I need one.

A   Complete the sentences with the words in parentheses and *be going to*.

1. _____*I'm going to change*_____ (I / change) my habits.

2. Whenever possible, _____ (I / not use) plastic.

3. _____ (It / not be) easy, but _____ (I / try).

4. Tomorrow, _____ (my roommate and I / go) shopping.

5. _____ (We / not buy) anything in plastic packaging.

6. Also, _____ (my friends / come) to my house this weekend.

7. _____ (We / not order) takeout* for dinner. That uses a lot of plastic.

8. _____ (We / make) our own dinner.

*****Takeout** is food you buy from a restaurant and then eat in another place.*

B   Complete each conversation. Use short answers where you can.

1. **A:** _____*Are you going to buy*_____ (you, buy) bottled water?

   B: No, _____.

   A: But you're thirsty. _____*What are you going to do*_____ (what, do)?

   B: I _____ (drink) water from the tap.

2. **A:** _____ (you, go) to the gym?

   B: Yes, _____.

   A: _____ (when, go)?

   B: _____ (after class).

3. **A:** _____ (Maria, go) to the gym with you?

   B: No, _____.

   A: _____ (what, do)?

   B: She _____ (study) in the library.

4. **A:** _____ (your parents, visit) this weekend?

   B: Yes, _____.

   A: _____ (where, they, stay)?

   B: They _____ (sleep) in my room.

   I _____ (sleep) on the couch.

HEALTH

LESSON A

IMPERATIVES			
Tell Someone to Do Something		**Tell Someone _Not_ to Do Something**	
Stay	calm.	**Don't panic.**	
Go	straight.	**Don't turn**	right.
Close	your eyes.	**Don't move**	your arms or legs.
Take	an aspirin every day.	**Don't forget**	to do it.
Use the imperative to give advice, directions, and orders.			
Add _please_ to make your request more polite. _Move outside, please._			

A Circle the correct answer to complete each sentence. Then compare your answers with a partner.

1. I feel sick. Please take _____.

   a. me to the doctor   b. some medicine

2. We're leaving for the airport. Don't _____ your passport.

   a. bring   b. forget

3. Shh! _____ quiet. _____ any noise.

   a. Don't be; Make   b. Be; Don't make

4. Does your eye hurt? Don't _____!

   a. rub it   b. put in eye drops

5. _____ the instructions again, please. I couldn't hear you the first time.

   a. Read   b. Don't read

6. It says, "Be careful! _____ this medicine on an empty stomach."

   a. Bring   b. Don't take

LESSON B

WHEN CLAUSES	
When Clause	**Result Clause**
When I drink coffee,	I can't sleep.
Result Clause	**When Clause**
I can't sleep	when I drink coffee.
The simple present is used in both the *when* clause and the result clause.	
The result clause can come first or second in a sentence. When it comes first, there is no comma between the two clauses.	

A Match each *when* clause with a result clause.

1. When I feel stressed,   a. people are usually nice to you.

2. When we argue,   b. I get hungry by 10:00.

3. When I sleep well,   c. my mom usually apologizes first.

4. When I don't eat breakfast,   d. I exercise.

5. When you're kind,   e. I'm late for class.

6. When I miss the bus,   f. I have a lot of energy.

B Rewrite the sentences in **A** so that the result clauses come first. Then tell a partner which sentences are true for you. Explain your answers.

1. _____

2. _____

3. _____

4. _____

5. _____

6. _____

C Compare your answers in **B** with a different partner.

11 ACHIEVEMENT

LESSON A

CAN AND *COULD* FOR ABILITY		
Subject	**Modal Verb**	**Base Form**	
I / You / He / She / We / They	**can** / can't **could** / couldn't	cook	well.

QUESTIONS AND SHORT ANSWERS				
Can	you	cook well?	Yes, I can.	No, I can't.
	he		Yes, he can.	No, he can't.
Could	you	cook well at age 16?	Yes, I could.	No, I couldn't.
	he		Yes, he could.	No, he couldn't.

Use *can* and *can't* to talk about things you are able or unable to do now.
  I **can** / **can't** cook well.

Use *could* and *couldn't* to talk about things you were able or unable to do in the past.
  I **could** / **couldn't** cook well at age 16.

Can, *can't*, *could*, and *couldn't* are the same for all subjects.
  I / Victor / They **can** cook well.

A Complete the sentences with *can*, *can't*, *could*, or *couldn't*.

1. As a young child, Hou Yifan _____ play chess well. She won many games.

2. Sorry, I _____ call you last night. I was busy, but I _____ talk to you now.

3. I'm so tired that I _____ stay awake.

4. When Ahmed was fifteen, he _____ speak two languages. Now, he speaks three.

5. Nicole _____ read music now, but two years ago she _____.

6. My dad always tells me, "You _____ succeed, but you have to work hard."

B Complete the exchanges. Write a question with *can* or *could*. Then write a short answer.

1. A: *Can you dance* _____?
   B: Yes, *I can* _____. I'm a very good dancer.

2. A: _____ with me today?
   B: Sorry, _____. I'm busy. Let's study tomorrow.

3. A: _____ a song in English?
   B: No, _____. Lena doesn't know any songs in English.

4. A: _____ French five years ago?
   B: _____. I spoke it fluently.

5. A: _____ when you were fifteen?
   B: _____. I was too young to drive.

CONNECTING IDEAS WITH *BECAUSE*	
Main Clause	**Reason Clause**
My family moved	**because** my dad got a new job.
Reason Clause	**Main Clause**
Because my dad got a new job,	my family moved.

Because can join two clauses together. A clause has a subject and a verb.

Because answers the question *why*. It gives a reason for an action.
  Why did your family move?
  (My family moved) because my dad got a new job.

In conversation, people often give the reason only (*Because my dad got a new job*). Don't do this in formal writing.

In writing, when the reason comes first, put a comma before the main clause.

CONNECTING IDEAS WITH *SO*	
Main Clause	**Result Clause**
My dad got a new job,	**so** my family moved.

So can join two clauses together.

So describes a result.

In writing, use a comma before *so* unless the two clauses are very short.

A Complete each sentence with *because* or *so*.

1. Many risk-takers are successful _____ they take chances.
2. My mom is afraid to fly, _____ she always drives places.
3. Smoking is dangerous, _____ Jon quit.
4. Bruno is nervous _____ he has a job interview.
5. I'm afraid to go to the dentist, _____ I hardly ever go.
6. Elena did well on the exam _____ she studied hard.
7. It was cold, _____ we didn't go to the beach.
8. I didn't understand a word, _____ I used my dictionary.
9. Everyone knows that video _____ it was popular last month.
10. Anh didn't like the movie _____ it was very long.

B Rewrite the five *because* sentences from **A** so the word *because* starts the sentence.

1. _____
2. _____
3. _____
4. _____
5. _____

C Unscramble the words to make sentences. Use commas if necessary.

1. don't / I / go rock climbing / it's / dangerous / because

_____

2. fly / so / the weather / bad / was / he / couldn't

_____

3. to fly / exciting / likes / it's / because / he

_____

4. the exam / I / failed / it / have to / retake / so / I

_____

12 AT THE MOVIES

LESSON A

THE PRESENT CONTINUOUS AS FUTURE			
Subject + *Be*	**Verb + *-ing***		**Future Time Expression**
We're	meeting	at the theater	at 8:00. in an hour. today / tonight / tomorrow.
I'm	going	to a movie	this weekend.
They're	releasing	the sequel	next year.

You can use the present continuous (often with a future time expression) to talk about future plans.
We're meeting at the theater in an hour.

Use the present continuous to talk about things you can plan (an appointment, a trip). Don't use it to talk about things you cannot plan (the weather, an illness). Do not say: *It's raining tomorrow.*
A: What **are** you **doing** this weekend?
B: **I'm going** to a movie on Saturday with friends.

A Complete the conversation. Use the present continuous and the words in parentheses. Also complete the time expressions with the words in the box.

> in   next   tomorrow

A: I heard that (1.) _____ (you / go) to Morocco. Is it for a new movie?

B: It is. (2.) _____ (the studio / make) a sci-fi film. (3.) _____ (we / shoot) part of it in Morocco.

A: (4.) _____ (when / you / leave)?

B: (5.) _____ at 6:00 a.m.
(6.) _____ (the crew / fly) together.
(7.) _____ (we / spend) a week in Spain. Then
(8.) _____ (we / go) to Morocco.

A: It sounds exciting. (9.) _____ (how long / you / stay)?

B: (10.) _____ (I / work) in Morocco for six weeks.
(11.) _____ (I / return) home at the end of
(12.) _____ month.

A: Sounds good. What about tomorrow? Do you need a ride to the airport?

B: Thanks, but (13.) _____ (a friend / drive) me
(14.) _____ the morning.

LESSON B

-ED ADJECTIVES	-ING ADJECTIVES
1a. I'm **bored**. I don't like this movie. **2a.** I was **surprised** by the ending.	**1b.** This movie is **boring**. Let's watch something else. **2b.** The end of the movie was **surprising**.

An *-ed* adjective describes a temporary feeling. Use it for people. In sentence 1a, *I'm bored* means "I feel bored."

An *-ing* adjective describes a feature of something or someone. It describes the cause of a feeling. Use it for people, things, or experiences. In sentence 1b, *This movie is boring* means "This movie is making me feel bored."

amazed / amazing bored / boring confused / confusing depressed / depressing	disappointed / disappointing entertained / entertaining excited / exciting exhausted / exhausting	frightened / frightening interested / interesting surprised / surprising

A Circle the correct words.

1. Action movies are **entertained / entertaining**, but their stories are not very **interested / interesting**.

2. That movie was so **excited / exciting**! I wasn't **bored / boring** at all.

3. I was **surprised / surprising** that the movie started at 1:00 and finished at 5:00. It was an **exhausted / exhausting** afternoon.

4. The story was **confused / confusing**, and the ending was **depressed / depressing**. Overall, I was **disappointed / disappointing** in the movie.

B Complete the sentences. Use the *-ed* or *-ing* adjective form of the word in parentheses.

Recently, I went sightseeing on a bus tour. We visited famous actors' homes. At first, I was (1.) _____ (excite) to go because I really like movies. I was (2.) _____ (interest) in seeing all of the expensive homes. Our tour guide told us funny and (3.) _____ (entertain) stories. But all of the homes had high walls and locked gates. We couldn't really see anything. It was (4.) _____ (disappoint). After three hours, I felt (5.) _____ (bore) and (6.) _____ (exhaust). Don't spend money on this tour. It's not worth it!

UNIT 2: LESSON B, VOCABULARY

nervous*

angry

happy

afraid

sad

bored

*__Nervous__ *is another word for* "worried."

UNIT 6: LESSON B, VOCABULARY

1. False. Most adults need to **sleep** seven or eight hours a night. Many teenagers need 9–10 hours.
2. True. When you follow the same schedule, you **sleep** better.
3. False. The light from a phone makes you **stay awake**. Read a book or magazine instead.
4. False. It's hard to **fall asleep** when you exercise a lot before bed.
5. False. Everyone **dreams**, but many people don't remember their dreams.
6. True. When you are **sleeping**, your brain is making memories so you can remember and learn. When you don't **sleep** well, it's easy to forget things.

UNIT 11: LESSON A, GRAMMAR

Student A: Answer your partner's questions about Ana. Use the information in the chart. Give short answers with *can*, *can't*, *could*, or *couldn't*. Put a (✓) for *yes* or an (✗) for *no*.

	Leo (Now)	Leo (3 years ago)	Ana (Now)	Ana (3 years ago)
Speak English			✓	✓
Cook well			✗	✗
Ride a bike			✓	✓
Dance			✓	✗
Stay up late			✗	✓

✓ = yes
✗ = no

❝ Can Ana speak English now?

Yes, she can. ❞

❝ Could she speak it three years ago?

Yes, she . . . ❞

You want to learn about Leo. Ask your partner questions with *can* and *could*.

UNIT 1

Where are you in the photo (in the mountains, in front of your house, etc.)? Tell your readers.

Connect words and sentences with the word *and*.

This is a photo of me and my father in 2013. We're in the mountains. In this photo, I'm ten years old, and my father is thirty-seven. He is tall and has dark hair and a beard. He's in great shape. These days, my father's hair is gray, and he's pretty heavy! In the photo, I'm kind of short, but now, I'm tall. Everyone says I look like my dad. What do you think?

UNIT 2

An object pronoun follows a verb or a preposition.

Question: Some people are afraid of dogs. Are you afraid of them? Explain.

Answer: No, dogs don't scare me. I have a dog, and he is very cute. His name is Sam, and everyone loves him.

OR

Answer: Yes, some dogs scare me. I'm afraid of them because they bite. Sometimes, dogs jump on you, too. I don't like that.

You can give a reason with *because*.

Question: When you speak English, how do you feel? Why?

Answer: Sometimes, I feel nervous because I don't understand everything. For example, sometimes the teacher talks to me, and I don't understand her. Then I feel a little nervous. Other times, I'm happy because I understand a lot. I'm trying to learn more so I can always understand people.

UNIT 3

In your first paragraph, tell your readers something interesting about your favorite store.

My favorite store is Uniqlo. The name *Uniqlo* comes from putting two words together: *unique* and *clothing*. I think it's a good name. The clothes at Uniqlo are stylish and different. You can wear them to school or the office, and they look great.

I'm a student, and I don't have a lot of money. I want to buy a new jacket. There's a jacket I like at the department store, but it's expensive. For the same amount of money, I can buy a jacket and a pair of pants at Uniqlo. That's why it's my favorite store!

In your second paragraph, write about one thing you want to buy there.

Finish with a sentence starting with *That's why...*

UNIT 4

Explain in the beginning why you are writing.

Hi Sofia and Angelo,

My grandmother and I are so excited to visit your city. I'm writing because I have a couple of questions.

I know that your city is very hilly. Is your apartment building on a steep hill? Is it possible to walk around the area easily? My grandmother is 80 years old. She's in good health, but she sometimes gets tired. Can you please give us some advice?

Thanks a lot,
Clarissa

When you write an informal email, you can use a casual greeting.

Use *is it possible...* to ask if you can do something.

Hi Clarissa,

Our building is at the bottom of a hill. You can easily walk to the beach on flat ground. When you need to go up the hill, you can take a taxi. Your grandmother should be fine.

See you on Saturday!

Safe travels,
Angelo

UNIT 5

Start your writing with *I nominate... for the Hero of the Year award*.

I nominate Zahara for the Hero of the Year award. Zahara is our neighbor, and I admire her a lot. She was our babysitter when my sister and I were little. She always played with us, and I loved spending time with her.

Use at least three adjectives to describe the person's personality.

Zahara is kind to me and my family. She is also very caring and generous with her time. She works in a hospital, and every day, she helps many people there. Last week, she stayed late and worked 12 hours every day. Sometimes, she's tired, but she always has a friendly smile.

Use the simple past to tell the reader what the person did.

Zahara likes to say, "Every stranger can become a new friend." Please consider her for the Hero of the Year award.

UNIT 6

At the start, say when the event happened. At the end, say how you felt.

Two weeks ago, I stayed up very late. I had to study for final exams. I started at 6:00 in the evening. At midnight, I took a break and drank some tea. Then I studied again. Finally, at 3:00 a.m., I went to bed, but I couldn't fall asleep. To relax, I listened to some music. Three hours later, my alarm rang. It was hard to wake up! I only slept for three hours, but I did really well on my two exams.

Use time expressions to tell the order of events.

UNIT 7

Use headings to separate your topics.

Getting from the airport to your hotel
There are many ways to get from the airport to your hotel. The traffic is usually heavy, so I think you should take the subway. In the airport, go straight to the elevators and down to the subway station on Level 1. There are many trains that go into the city.

Sightseeing
I think you should start with a city bus tour. You can buy your ticket online. Then get on the bus at the bus station across from the library. The bus stops at all the famous museums, parks, and bridges. The bus driver gives you a lot of information about each sight. You can get on and off the bus many times with the same ticket.

Tell your reader how to find important locations by using words like *across*, *in*, *next to*, and *on the corner of*.

UNIT 8

Use *most people say that I'm . . .* to talk about your personality.

Most people say that I'm friendly and easy-going. I like to try new things and meet new people. I'm also a very active* person. In my free time, I like to be outside.

These days, I'm preparing to run a half-marathon. I wake up at 5:00 a.m. and go running four times a week. Sometimes it's hard, but I love it. In the evenings, I need some quiet time. I usually play video games or study. Once in a while, I cook and invite my friends over. We eat and watch movies. It's a lot of fun.

Use *in my free time . . .* to tell people about your interests.

*If you're **active**, you have a lot of energy and move your body a lot.*

UNIT 9

In the second and third paragraphs, introduce your goal with the words *first* and *second*.

Next, state the problem. (*Most people use these things once…*)

Use *instead* to explain your change.

End the paragraph by saying why the change is good.

Plastic is a big problem, but we can do many things to use less. Here are my two goals.

First, I'm not going to buy drinks in plastic bottles or cups. Most people use these things once, and then they put them in the trash. Instead, I'm going to buy a reusable bottle. I can put many different drinks in it—water, tea, coffee, and juice. Then I can use less plastic, and I can save money, too.

Second, I'm going to eat less takeout food. Twice a week, I get takeout for lunch, and I use plastic cups, spoons, and bags. Instead, I'm going to bring my lunch. This way, I can use less plastic, and I can eat a healthy meal.

Are these changes going to help? I don't know, but I'm going to try. We have to start somewhere.

UNIT 10

I don't have a lot of stress in my life. I'm pretty easy-going, but sometimes, I worry about passing my exams and getting a good job. I know I can't control the future, but I still think about it. When I'm really stressed, I feel tired. My eyes hurt from looking at the computer screen. It's hard to focus on my schoolwork.

> Be specific about how stress makes you feel.

> What is a challenge you face? How do you handle it? Tell the reader about it.

When I have a lot of stress, I try to find a quiet place. That's hard to do. I have a brother and a sister, and it's noisy at home. Usually, I go to my room and close the door. Then I put on headphones and listen to my favorite music. I just try to relax. When I do that, I usually feel better after only a few minutes. It helps a lot.

UNIT 11

> State your goal at the start.

In the future, I want to move to Santiago. Right now, I live with my family in a small city in northern Chile. My life is very comfortable, but it's also a little boring.

> Give two reasons for your goal and explain each.

I want to live in Santiago because it's a big city, and there's a lot to do. Also, Santiago is the capital of Chile, so there are more jobs there. Maybe I can even start a business. I want to take a chance and try.

> How do you plan to reach your goal? Explain in the last paragraph.

I'd like to move after college, but first, I have to save some money. That's a little difficult because I don't have a job yet. But I'm very ambitious, and I'm good at planning and saving. Wish me luck!

UNIT 12

> You don't have to know all the details exactly. Do your best!

Cinema Paradiso is a classic film. A lot of the story takes place in a small town in the 1940s or 1950s. It's about an Italian boy named Salvatore and an older man named Alfredo. Alfredo works in the movie theater. Salvatore loves movies, and he gets a part-time job at the theater. The movie is about Salvatore's life. We see him as a little boy, a teenager, and an adult.

> Your readers may not know your movie. Tell them the basic story.

I like the scenes inside the movie theater because they're funny. I also like the ending. It's sad but also beautiful. Some people think this movie is boring, but I think it's a wonderful and sweet film.

> How do you feel about the movie? How do others feel? Present both opinions.

CREDITS